CAMPAIGN CHRONICLES

A journal of conversations on my wild
US Senate campaign all over Arizona

By Deedra Abboud

Foreword by Tara Ijai
Founder of the Love Glasses Revolution

Campaign Chronicles

A journal of conversations on my wild US Senate
campaign all over Arizona

As You Wish Publishing, LLC
Connect@asyouwishpublishing.com

ISBN-13: 978-1-951131-14-2

Library of Congress Control Number: 2021901481

Printed in the United States of America.

Nothing in this book or any affiliations with this book is a
substitute for medical or psychological help. If you are
needing help please seek it.

Cover graphic by Chris Ayers Creative

First and foremost, I thank my husband for his consistent support and encouragement in everything I do.

I also thank Tara Ijai, who has always been the best bestie ever imagined and turned "campaign cheerleader" into a tangible staff position that will be forever desired by anyone running for office.

Thank you Delos Nokleby for #ItsAbboudTime

Last but not least, I thank all my supporters in all my endeavors of making the world a better place, including my two political campaigns.

I truly couldn't have done anything without all of you just being you and being you in my circle.

Thank you.

Love is the marriage of strength & compassion.

Table of Contents

Foreword

Fearless. That's how I see her. I've known Deedra Abboud for about 18 years now. We are best friends. How did we meet, you ask? Oh, well now that's a whole other story, and it depends if you ask her or me what version you get.

She is all of 5'2", petite and adorable and can usually be found rocking a bright, colorful headscarf. She speaks with the most adorable Southern accent, confusing people on where she's from. Often times they would never guess Arkansas.

She's always thinking, processing and analyzing. She's got this huge computer brain, and conversations are anything but predictable when speaking with Deedra. If you ever have the pleasure of speaking with her, you would recognize she doesn't speak "off the cuff." Her responses are wise and well-thought-out statements that leave you thinking. If you were to speak with Deedra, you would instantly recognize her wisdom and intellect, which, to be fair, can even intimidate someone like me that loves to mostly joke about everything.

I mean, don't get me wrong, she jokes, but even her jokes are well thought out. I recall saying something really random one time at a restaurant, and we sat in what was (for me) an awkward silence for what seemed like an eternity.

In reality, it was like one minute, and just as I was getting ready to say something else to break the silence, she responded. She came up with some jaw-dropping wisdom, or sometimes in other situations, she would hold you accountable by drilling down deeper by asking questions and almost forcing you to think beyond your statement that you made. You see, her investigator type personality and her computer-like brain had been over there analyzing my random statement, and she had no concern over the awkward 1-minute silence. Hell, I don't even think she was aware of it because her mind was working. It is ALWAYS working.

I could give you other inklings of her "process." That's what I call her computer-like brain. We would go to a restaurant and order, and it would never be random. Nothing she does is random. There are built-in calculations. I can't even call them rules because they are not set, they are always variable, but they are there. There is not one damn thing that she has not thought through. From using a straw, to what drink to order for what meal, for what order the food should be delivered based on so many things that she has already worked through without you ever knowing it. She does not limit this capability to just herself. She is willing and happy to share her process with you, but she will never tell you what to do. She just gives all the options she has thought about and even some potential consequences of what those options might cause.

I had not been a person who thought in that capacity. I'm a feeler, so I use a lot of intuition and gut feelings and often times cannot put into words easily what I want to say. This is what made our friendship so damn yin and yang. We were so completely different that we complemented each other perfectly.

Deedra has always been involved in advocacy work. She was a civil rights advocate; a community leader, and her heart has always been in helping the underdog. In 2017 when it was a particularly challenging year in politics, especially for minority groups, Deedra announced to me she was going to run for the US Senate in Arizona. I recall saying, "Yeah, you should do it!" Little did I know she wanted me to help out or what that would even entail. She wanted me to be her wingman. I remember thinking, "What did we get into?" I knew nothing about politics or about this process.

I was absolutely sure that she was out of her mind because I was certain to say something wrong or do something wrong. I will never forget the words she said to me when I expressed my fears. She looked right into my eyes and said, "I just need you to be you."

She gave me the title of Official Campaign Cheerleader, and it was one of the most amazing experiences of my lifetime. Once Deedra planted the seed that I was an asset to her campaign, I almost began to believe it. She had a vision that I couldn't even see yet. All I knew was that I just had to be me and do what it is that I already love to do, hype up my friends in the most authentic way possible. I learned that I really love telling her story through social media and reaching not only her base, but anyone who wanted to learn about Deedra Abboud. I learned so much more about Deedra being by her side for 18 months, traveling all over the state of Arizona and the country together.

I watched in awe as she handled "haters" with dignity, class and grace. I watched her have some of the most incredibly difficult conversations with ease. She was never invested in changing people's minds. That was never the goal. She has always been about planting seeds. She often says she is not responsible if the seeds grow because she's not the sun, the rain, or the soil. Her job is only to plant the seeds, and what comes will come.

She also reframed my whole life when she spoke of defining success. You see, most politicians would gauge success based on how much money they raised, and while we understood the importance of that, Deedra reminded us of what a "win" looked like along our campaign trail. It was the teenager dressed like Deedra and after speaking with her now wants to run for office; it was meeting people all over the state of Arizona and many of who we are still connected to today, and it was showing people that a US Senate campaign could be run with total transparency.

What I want to share with you, the reader, is that this book is a compilation of very real conversations that occurred on the campaign trail. She posted these conversations on social media, and they became very popular. We received feedback daily about these conversations and how inspirational they were to followers. People loved to see the way Deedra handled conversations on the campaign and how to engage with people using civil discourse. She taught us how to never mistake kindness for weakness.

You see, I get to have access to my bestie all the time, I get the pleasure of experiencing her "process," and I am very excited that you now get to experience it too. I don't mind sharing her with you. Will everyone think like Deedra? Of course not, and you shouldn't! You just have to be YOU.

FOREWORD

However, each person can look at the unique points of view that she brings to a conversation that helps you think outside of yourself and question your own beliefs or the way you think about something.

She has an amazing gift and thought process, and I couldn't be more elated that you get to enjoy it too.

May you all use your own gifts and talents to continue making the world a better place.

Tara Ijai

Founder, Love Glasses Revolution

"Choosing To See The World With Love"

Preface

Like many great things in life, the #Campaign Chronicles were an extraordinary accident. I often write down conversations I've had as a means to reflect.

What was really going on in the conversation?

Could I have responded better?

What was the lesson?

One day while on the campaign trail, I had some conversations with protestors that even blew *my* mind.

I decided to share a couple of them on Facebook without thought of strategy or outcomes. Just sharing.

They practically went viral with both comments and reactions.

As my entire campaign strategy was around having real conversations about things that mattered – though at the time I was focused on policy issues as the "things that mattered" – I immediately recognized the value of sharing with the public all those individual conversations I was having and documenting for my own use.

And thus, the #CampaignChonicles were born and incorporated for both my own social media and the campaign.

People found them entertaining.

People found them inspiring.

People found them frustrating.

People found them shocking.

People found them informative.

I found them to be great conversation starters.

Which was always my point.

We can't solve problems if we never talk about them. And we can't solve problems if we only talk about them in our bubbles, never hearing other perspectives.

But not everyone wants to be involved in uncomfortable conversations.

The #CampaignChronicles gave many front row seats as watchers, a place where they could witness the uncomfortable… so they could then reflect on the issues and perspectives without being in an uncomfortable situation themselves.

The watchers are always my target audience. They make up a large chunk of the so-called "silent majority."

They're rarely vocal about their perspectives outside their immediate social circles, and often not even there, but they are engaged intellectually. They're thinking about things, sometimes quite deeply, quietly, and in private.

When we forfeit conversations on things that matter, when we avoid pushback, even simple "That's not true" statements, mistakenly believing we're taking the high road, going along to get along, we allow false information to spread as truth.

Because if it were untrue, wouldn't someone say so?

PREFACE

We can have conversations without allowing them to turn into arguments, most of the time.

Because conversations shouldn't be about winning or changing people's minds.

They're about the exchange of ideas and finding common ground... or at least they should be.

I've included some tips at the beginning of each chapter to [hopefully] do just that.

My hope is that you find the tips and chronicles both entertaining and helpful in your journey to have more productive conversations about things that matter.

The only "winning" in my estimation is holding on to your values and standing in your own power when challenged.

My values are honesty (to myself above all), creativity (there is always a way), and instruction (sharing knowledge).

I also believe "being nice" is over-rated and kindness is what we should strive for – while understanding kindness is not the same as "nice."

Often, for me, kindness is simply keeping the person on topic, asking questions to get to the root of the matter, not making personal attacks, and not reacting to personal attacks.

You will find some of the conversations start out the same way but end up going in a different direction. That's usually how conversations work.

It's not about having the "perfect answer."

It's about interacting with the individual at a specific time and place, recognizing their energy, where they are, where you are, and where you have the potential to go.

And that changes daily, sometimes hourly.

Be Brave

There is no better advice I could give any person for every aspect of their lives than to know yourself.

I often joke that I have a Ph.D. in Deedra. I spent decades very focused on finding out who I am and what makes me tick. That knowledge has helped me make quicker and better decisions because I know my values, I know my strengths and weaknesses, I know my passions, I know what I do not like, and I know what I will not tolerate as well as what will trigger me to abandon all my good intentions.

And even more importantly, I can hear my inner voice telling me when something doesn't feel right.

After years of practice, I can usually recognize what someone is trying to accomplish in a conversation with me, such as manipulation.

At the very least, I can recognize, in the moment, that they're not interested in connecting with me or truly discussing the issue at hand.

But the first step requires an intimate knowledge of me.

The more I know myself, the more I can filter out my own baggage from the situation I'm facing – so that I can focus on the situation instead of my own confusion or frustration.

So, take the time to get to know you.

The more you dig, the more interesting and amazing you will find you are.

And the less other people and situations will confuse you.

That is where you'll find your true grit, your very own personal power of bravery.

Woman: What advice would you give women who might think about running for office?

Me: Know yourself very well. Know your boundaries. Know what about you you're willing to compromise and what you're not. All three will be tested.

Woman: "When they go low, we go high" isn't working.

Me: I would suggest it's the misunderstanding of what "going high" means that isn't working.

Woman: What do you mean?

Me: Going high doesn't mean ignoring stuff. It means facing it head-on with the strength of our character and not letting them pull us down to their level.

Woman: How do we do that?

Me: Start with knowing you, knowing your own character. Start with knowing your boundaries, actually having and enforcing your own boundaries. Start with using "No" as a complete sentence that ends in a period, without explanation.

Woman: Aren't you scared traveling all over Arizona?

Me: Why?

Woman: Aren't you afraid people will attack you in the rural areas?

Me: I've never had a negative experience outside the cities. People in rural areas are always nice and courteous, even the very few protestors I can count on one hand.

Woman: Really?! I would have thought it would be worse there.

Me: Nope. I had one guy yell at me in Tucson from a distance, and he didn't even know I was running for office, and several follow me around Maricopa County for their Facebook Live videos. Never happened in the rural areas.

Woman: That's good to hear.

Me: People trying to whip up the hate, like Milo, only go to cities. They never go to rural areas. That's something to think about when we're talking about where the hate is.

Man: What do you think about the current civility debate?

Me: People not being civil are lecturing the rest of us on civility. Civil doesn't mean docile.

Woman: It's making me so mad that the media is ignoring you and pushing the other candidate like it's a done deal.

Me: I've moved from the "Muslim Candidate" to "the other woman." That's progress in my book.

Woman: But it's not fair!

Me: Who said politics is fair? I'm earning every vote the old-fashioned way... actually talking to people. We're shaking up 2018, and they won't be able to ignore us once I'm on the ballot!

BE BRAVE

Woman: Is Donald Trump your president?!

Me: Yes. That's how elections in a Democracy works.

Woman: Then, you need to shut up and support him!

Me: Support is earned. Elected office is a privilege. And only dictators get blind support without criticism.

Woman: You're not a patriot! You need to get out of our country if you can't support our president!

Me: A true patriot defends the Constitution and our principles, not individuals blindly. My patriotism is on point.

Reporter: We're seeing more candidates from both parties refusing to be interviewed unless they receive the questions beforehand and can control the story. McSally even kicked a reporter out of an event. What do you think of that?

Me: It's undemocratic and reeks of dishonesty. I'm able to engage with Nationalist Patriots, and I'm fairly certain that's way harder than dealing with questions from reporters and constituents, even unfriendly ones.

Woman: We have to have candidates that can reach across the aisle.

Me: I agree. As an attorney, I intimately understand compromise, which involves two sides giving and taking. If Democrats are the only ones reaching and promoting reaching, that's not a compromise. More importantly, in any negotiation, you must understand your bottom line, what you will not negotiate or give up.

Woman: What's not negotiable to you?

Me: Corporate money in politics. Subsidizing the fossil-fuel industry while sabotaging the alternative energy industry. Giving tax breaks to major profitable corporations instead of small businesses, which are the ultimate equalizer between rural and urban areas. Allowing corporations to commoditize people in healthcare, education, and criminal justice. The United States government putting kids in cages. Ignoring entire communities because they're not a major voting bloc. That's just off the top of my head.

Protestor: Why are you upset?

Me: I'm not upset. I'm passionate. But I understand a strong, passionate woman is confusing to some people.

Woman 1 [Black]: You have to be careful and not show too much passion, or they'll accuse you of being an angry Black woman.

Woman 2 [Black]: [frustrated groan]

Me: I disagree.

Woman: You don't understand because you're not a Black woman.

Me: No, but I'm a woman. And I know that the angry woman accusation has been used to take away our power and force us to make ourselves smaller for generations. It's time we stopped accepting the accusation as true.

Woman 1: We're not accepting it as true. We're accepting the reality that it will be used against us.

Me: It's used against us even when we're not mad. And if it's not that, it's something else. I also notice that the reminder is almost always given by women to women. What would happen if we women, as allies, stood with each other and pushed back on the accusation instead of encouraging our sisters to conform to the well-documented method of keeping women quiet and powerless?

Woman 2: That will take generations.

Woman 1: And it has consequences.

Me: Everything has consequences. I'm focused on the reward. Playing small and by antiquated rules does us more harm than good. We need to stop asking for permission to be our best selves. And we need to do it now.

Protestor 1 [armed]: Why are you against teachers being armed in schools to protect our children?

Me: The teacher's job is to teach our children. They're not security guards. No one can predict what a person will do with a gun in an emergency situation, even with training.

Protestor 2 (woman with child): I would expect a teacher to protect my children!

Me: Teachers will die for your children. Some already have. Just adding guns to the classroom and expecting teachers to shoot someone, maybe even a child they know, in an emergency situation, is not enough to solve the mass shooting problem.

Protestor 2 [armed]: Not all the teachers should be armed. Just some of them. And they would be trained.

Me: Wouldn't it be nice if all people who had guns had training? Why teachers and no one else?

[Protestor 2 walks away]

Protestor 1: The Second Amendment is in the Constitution. What part of 'cannot be infringed' don't you understand?

Bystander: What do you think Amendment means? It means 'a change.'

[Protestor 1 has a look of confusion]

Me: All rights can be restricted. You can't yell 'fire' in a crowded theater as freedom of speech. You can't purchase every weapon ever made without restriction. You can be convicted of a crime that removes your Constitutional right to purchase or own a weapon.

Protestor 1: But you can file to get your rights back.

Me: Yes, a process. A restriction that can be approved or denied.

Protestor: What part of 'shall not infringe' don't you understand?

Me: The part where US Courts have already ruled that the government can legally restrict some weapons for public safety without it being a Constitutional infringement.

Woman: You converted me tonight, but I'd like to ask how your funding is going.

Me: Well, I don't have $5 million, but... if the middle class continues to shrink, if we continue to let people go bankrupt because they can't afford healthcare, if we're going to have to continue donating to non-profits that are forced to take over all the social safety nets the government is abdicating, there's not going to be anyone left to donate to politicians. We'd better figure out how to reach donors and excite them enough to vote for us without $5 million soon... or big donors and corporations will be the only ones controlling our elections. Our campaign is showing how that's done. Right now.

Being Positively Intolerant

I believe we need more pushback in our lives.

Boundaries are the foundation of pushback. What will we tolerate, and what will we not tolerate?

We teach people how to treat us by how we treat ourselves and how we allow others to treat us.

Next comes how we allow others to treat others in our presence.

And then what we allow others to witness of our tolerance of behaviors toward us and others.

We often look at the events of the world and are outraged, but then allow the papercuts to happen unabated in our own circles of influence – home, work, social groups.

We can't influence the world if we can't influence within our own circles of influence.

And it all begins with knowing you, knowing your values, creating your boundaries, and then enforcing them.

One step at a time. One conversation at a time. One person at a time.

Woman [Muslim]: I wanted to let you know I was at a women's party, and they were talking about your campaign. They said they think you are too flashy in your dress with all the color and you are too close to men in your pictures.

Me: Did they have a problem with any of my policies?

Woman: I don't think your policies came up.

Me: So, it was just gossip.

Woman: No. They were really concerned about the image you are giving about Muslims and especially about how much you're disrespecting your husband.

Me: I feel pretty good about the image I'm giving about Muslims, and my husband would be very offended by their fake outrage on his behalf.

Woman: You're not listening to me. I'm trying to help you by letting you know what people are saying about you.

Me: Oh, I'm listening to you. I'm just not seeing where I'm the one in the wrong.

Woman [Muslim]: I wanted to let you know there's a lot of talk among Muslims that you need to be more modest in your dress and behavior. Not me. I just listened. But I wanted you to know.

Me: What would be really helpful to me and all women in the world, not to mention Islam and humanity, is if you stopped the judgmental gossip when you hear it... or at least recognize it for what it is.

Man: I was following that crazy conversation you were having on Facebook today. Why did you keep answering her? You need to learn to just walk away.

Me: I ignore stuff all the time. But some things are too important to walk away from. They need to see we will push back and not let them control the narrative.

Man: But you'll never win with these people. It's a waste of time.

Me: The post you're talking about was with a self-professed liberal, feminist, social justice advocate, and environmentalist... not a right-wing conservative. Having the conversations in our own camp is even more important.

Man: But you didn't convince her.

Me: It was never about convincing her. It was about not letting her bully others with her opinion, which was clearly her intent. It was also about letting others have comfortable front row seats to witness a controversial conversation... so they can see perspectives around the issue and hopefully come to a conclusion themselves.

Woman: When I talk to other Democrats about you, they bring up sharia, that you're a terrorist and stuff.

Me: Do you point out the absurdity?

Woman: No. I support your [Democratic] opponent.

Me: I remember McCain at a town hall where a lady started saying Obama was not an American, was a Muslim, and was a terrorist. McCain set her straight about his opponent. That's character. That's supposed to be who we are as Democrats.

Protestor: All you Muslims want to kill us!

Me: The reality that 150k Muslims live in Arizona and aren't killing anybody isn't proof to the contrary?

Muslim: Why don't you talk more about Islam in your campaign? You have the opportunity to teach so many people about Islam.

Me: How about we try living Islam instead of just talking about it?

Muslim: I can't find a rally against the Muslim ban. You should create one.

Me: There's a family separation rally this week.

Woman: That's not the same.

Me: It is to me. We'll fight all the attacks together, or we'll get interned and deported separately. I choose together.

Man: You know Arizonans won't vote for you because of your name.

Me: Deedra?

Man: No. Abboud [pronounced Abood]

Me: You know Arizonans already voted for someone with my name... Paula Aboud [pronounced Abood]

Man: Oh.

Reporter: So, you're running for US Senate, and you're Muslim.

Me: Yes. Every day.

Reporter: Tell me about the scarf.

Me: Sure. I'd rather talk about people dying cause they don't have healthcare or how not protecting Net Neutrality is a threat to our freedom, but I understand a female candidate's clothing is always just so important to the American people.

Man: A [teacher] strike is not the answer!

Me: What is the answer?

Man: They can march in the summer.

Me: The budget is being discussed by the legislature now, and they won't do so again until next year. How do you apply pressure when there's no school, and the legislature is on vacation?

Man: They can vote in November!

Me: I think they will. But voting is only half of the solution, and it's no solution when our legislators think they have all the power... which appears to be the problem from Phoenix to D.C.

Woman: The whole teacher strike thing is stupid. Teachers are supposed to be there for the kids, not to get rich.

Me: You think teachers are being greedy?

Woman: Absolutely! A lot of people have low pay in the US, and you don't see them threatening to strike!

Me: That's because we have systematically dismantled Unions. People don't have the ability or power to strike or even collectively negotiate anymore.

Woman: They don't need to. You should better negotiate your own wages when you're hired. That's on the individual.

Me: That would be great, except most people are more focused on getting a job. They need to eat and pay their bills. If the wages offered are too low, too many are forced to take it... along with two or three other jobs to make ends meet.

Woman: We live in a free country. If they don't like the job or the wages, they can get a different job.

Me: And that's what many are doing. We have more qualified teachers not teaching in Arizona than job openings... and we have almost as many unfilled positions as filled positions. They're leaving the profession in droves. Arizona is so desperate for teachers, we've reduced teacher qualification requirements.

Woman: Anyway, it's not my problem because my kids are grown.

Me: I don't have kids, and it still concerns me. If we keep reducing the pay, qualifications, and professional respect for teachers while pushing kids out of school through privatization, we will become a failed state. That's a proven fact you can read about in some of the dilapidated history books in our schools. I don't want that to happen in my lifetime or after I'm gone.

Man: If they [teachers] want more money, they need to change jobs.

Me: Many are. Right out of teaching. We have over 2,000 vacancies in Arizona due to that.

Man: I wish my job paid more, but you don't see me demanding that or threatening to strike.

Me: It's not a wage competition. Teachers are standing up for themselves, the support staff, and the kids. How long do you think we can prosper as a country with school buildings falling apart, outdated textbooks, and a fleeing workforce?

Man: What should I say when my fellow Democrats say they won't vote for a Muslim?

Me: Ask them if they just have a Muslim bias or if it includes other marginalized groups. Then remind them that Democratic values are supposed to include everyone.

Protestor: If we don't limit immigration, we'll soon be a minority!

Me: So, you're saying being a minority in America is a bad thing?

Protestor: This is our country! We can't let immigrants change that!

Me: Was your family Native American or immigrants? Just so I know where to go with this....

Man: Asking for healthcare for all is just too progressive.

Me: I would argue that healthcare for all is a moderate position these days. People, regardless of party affiliation, are recognizing they don't want to die because they can't pay for chronic illness treatments for themselves or their families.

Woman [Muslim]: The [Muslim] brother over there [pointing] wanted me to tell you that you're not dressed modestly.

Me: Tell the brother over there that if he lowered his gaze like the religion says, he wouldn't know what I'm wearing... and it would continue to be none of his business.

Man: Can you explain Islam to me?

Me: I'm running for a political office, not a religious position. We can talk about how important the separation of religion and state is, though.

Reporter: We'd like to interview you about your campaign. Can we meet you at one of the local Mosques?

Me: There are 23 Mosques in Maricopa County, but is there a reason we need to meet at a Mosque?

Reporter: We were just thinking of a good backdrop.

Me: Do you ask other candidates to meet at their religious institutions?

Reporter: No.

Me: Where do you meet them?

Reporter: Offices, coffee shops, our studios...

Me: All of those sound good to me...

Man [Muslim]: How come we don't see your husband with you on the campaign trail?

Me: Cause he's not running for office. But he travels for business a lot too.

Man: Oh, you have one of those modern marriages where you live separate lives. I will never understand that.

Me: Men have been traveling away from their families since the beginning of time... world exploration, spreading religious messages, conquering the world, traveling merchants.... I'm not sure what's modern about that, except now we have great technology to keep us connected.

Clarity Rules

I'm a person of few words. I like to get to the point. I prefer clarity over all things. It reduces confusion.

I find most people are unclear – both in their own understanding of issues and in their speech around issues.

Say what you mean and mean what you say is one of my personal mottos.

Most people interpret that as being only about keeping your word.

I see it much bigger.

To me, it's knowing yourself enough to know what you value, what you believe, what you will tolerate, and what you want.

If you know those things intimately, you can be much clearer in expressing them, living them, and having conversations around them.

Knowledge is power, and there is no greater power than being grounded in your knowledge of you.

The rest is just useful information.

Woman: I'm not into politics.

Me: Yet politics is so into you!

Woman: I stay way out of politics.

Me: But politics is so into you. Soon it will make all your bodily decisions for you.

Man 1: I'm against abortion... but I don't think the government should be involved in it. That's for the women to decide.

Me: If it were only about abortion, we could have that discussion. But it's not. It's about controlling women's sexuality. Lately, it's about whether women can even have birth control access.

Woman: What do you mean?

Me: The Hobby Lobby case was completely about your employer deciding whether you can have birth control through your insurance. That's completely against any free-market argument – your employer deciding what medical procedures your insurance company can offer you based solely on your employer's religious beliefs and not yours.

Man 2 [to Man 1]: Will you let me have birth control through our insurance? [both men laugh]

Me: Oh, don't worry. Men's bodies don't have any regulating laws at all.

Woman: None of that is fair!

Me: No, it isn't. But as long as you're proud to stay out of politics, that unfairness will continue. Primarily for women, mind you.

Woman [Muslim]: You shouldn't be running.

Me: Why not?

Woman: Because Muslim women shouldn't be in leadership.

Me: Wasn't Khadijah a major merchant and business owner?

Woman: Yes.

Me: Didn't Ayesha lead a battle?

Woman: Yes.

Me: I think I'm good then.

Woman: But that was a different time, and they were with the Prophet.

Me: Actually, no. Khadijah had her business both before and after joining the Prophet, even hired him as her employee. Ayesha led the battle after his death. The religion is fairly clear on women's liberation. It's culture that's messed up.

Woman: I heard you on a podcast where you brought up the unpaved highways on Navajo lands. You really shouldn't talk about stuff like that if you don't know how the Navajo feel about it.

Me: I actually have spoken to many Navajo about it and can even tell you why the highways still aren't paved.

Woman: But it's just not an issue you should be addressing. It's up to them.

Me: Can you imagine a scenario where the Navajo would want unpaved roads that put their lives in danger every day?

Woman: They probably don't want outsiders coming in to pave their roads.

Me: Nope. That's definitely not it. They've been begging for their roads to be paved and help with their erosion problem for years.

Me: Hi! I'm Deedra, running for US Senate.

Man: You're not the Libertarian candidate, are you?

Me: No. Both the Libertarian and Green candidates didn't make the ballot. Just the two Party choices.

Man: Well, I'm Independent, so I'm excluded in the primary.

Me: Oh no. Only the presidential primary. You are welcome in every other primary. You just have to request a party ballot.

Man: Oh, ya. I forgot that. But it's too late now.

Me: Nope. You have until August 17th to request a mail ballot. Or you can just go into any Ballot Center and vote between now and August 28th.

Man: Wow! Imagine that. An organized government!

Me: Yes! We're working on getting more of that!

Note: Arizona's primary is now the first Tuesday in August.

Man: It made me mad to see all those teachers marching at the Capitol for higher pay. Why are they not marching for the kids to be safe at schools? That's more important than their pay.

Me: They were not just marching for higher pay. They were marching for the schools to be better funded to serve the kids. That's not just their pay so we can have qualified teachers staying in the profession but also money for books, supplies, buildings that aren't falling apart, and more school counselors.

Man: Oh. I didn't understand that. I support them then!

Me: And that's what we all need from you.

Woman: The Pima County Superior Court and their investigators are ruining mine and others' lives with their corruption. What will you do as a future Senator to stop the corruption in Pima County?

Me: I believe we can improve the lives of more Arizonans if elected leaders on all levels work together and communicate more. Which is why I make it a point to know every person running for office in Arizona this year. But I'm running for a Federal Office. As a Senator, my ability to end corruption, which I have prioritized by signing contracts such as #CandidatesWithAContract, is mostly limited to the federal level.

Woman: I have a specific issue with the lack of Black representation in the arts and exhibitions in Phoenix. What will you do about that as Senator?

Me: I'm running for a federal office where I can focus on stopping the current disregard of the arts in general as well as the lack of inclusion of people of color in all public spaces. My plan is to draw attention to the issues facing Arizonans and working more with other elected offices on those issues. Elected leaders on all levels should see each other as resources, not competitors.

Man: What do you call what you wear on your head?

Me: A scarf.

Man: I thought it had an Arabic name.

Me: It has lots of names in different languages, but it's just a scarf in English.

Man: Oh. Ok.

Man: It's not realistic to decriminalize cannabis on the federal level.

Me: Why not?

Man: Because then how would you stop it from being imported?

Me: That would be customs. There are many things you can possess or bring into the US but can't import for the purpose of selling. Pharmaceuticals come to mind. In fact, there are drugs that are illegal to sell in the US and illegal to import for selling, but you can still personally bring in for personal use.

Note: Arizona voters legalized the purchase and possession of small amounts of cannabis in 2020.

Me: We need to decriminalize cannabis on the federal level.

Man: The Republicans will never let that happen.

Me: John Boehner has joined the cannabis industry as a spokesperson for legalization.

Man: Oh....

Me: Yes, the landscape is changing. The people and political support are there. We just need to elect people willing to push for it and do it.

Woman 1: You said you believe in Healthcare for all. Does that include single payer?

Me: Yes.

Woman 2: No. Medicare for all is better.

Me: How is that different?

Woman 3: I don't like Medicare. Medicaid for all is better.

[All three start arguing with each other]

Me: Ok. Ok. You see why I say Healthcare for all? Let's agree we want everyone to have healthcare, quality healthcare, instead of bankruptcy and death, and work on that instead of arguing over the label. If we are all dedicated to the same goal, we can figure out the details... maybe even a system no one has thought of before. That used to be what the United States was known for.

Man: What will people do if Congress does do away with Social Security?

Me: That's a good question. A lot of people will become homeless, go hungry, and maybe even die.

Man: I heard even some Democrats voted to take money away from Social Security. Don't they understand what that will do to the people?

Me: It boggles the mind, doesn't it? They're definitely not thinking long-term or in our best interests.

Woman: I contacted all my Congressional Representatives, and they all replied they don't know what to do [about mass shootings] or that there was nothing they could do.

Me: Not even enforcing the current law? Mandatory updating of the database for people who have lost their Constitutional right to possess weapons due to conviction seems fairly non-controversial. Maybe requiring all gun sales are checked against that database because the law is clear about their loss of a Constitutional right. It's not that they can't figure out what to, it's that they don't want to do anything.

Man: What's your stance on the death penalty?

Me: As long as our Criminal Justice System is executing innocent people, we cannot morally back state-sponsored executions. Even one innocent death should be concerning, but we're well beyond just one.

Man: Yes!

Me: And that's not even getting into the number of innocent people convicted or forced into plea deals because they can't afford to fight for their freedom.

Woman: Telephones have always been luxury items; cell phones haven't changed that. If people want them, they need to plan their finances better.

Me: Few people have home phones, and payphones are almost non-existent. 911 and Amber Alerts are 100% dependent on cell phones. Never mind getting the news, being connected to the world, or calling a friend to talk you out of suicide. Cell phones are a necessity today, maybe even more important than housing. You can sleep on a couch if you have a phone to call a friend.

Woman: Business owners are being hurt by the frivolous lawsuits over ADA compliance.

Me: People with disabilities are being hurt because they can't access public spaces.

Woman: But it costs us money to make those accommodations. We can't afford it!

Me: It costs you money to have the required number of bathrooms, parking spaces, and proper temperatures for food too. All that is for public safety, as is the ADA.

Woman: The new law will give us more time to comply and have a mediation process.

Me: HR620 simply allows businesses to wait and see if they will be caught not complying and forces an already disadvantaged community to do all the work to enforce an already existing civil rights law that's been around since the 1980s.

Woman: I like the things you're telling me, but I also like what Trump is doing. What do you think about Trump?

Me: The administration seems to be thriving on chaos, and we could definitely use more calm in the storm.

Woman: Yes. If he'd just stop talking and tweeting. And those kids... at least they're trying to get them back to their families now.

Me: It does boggle the mind that we keep better records of confiscated property than we did when we took those kids from their parents.

Woman: I know. I just can't believe people were so irresponsible. Some people should lose their jobs over this.

Me: Yes. Total lack of long-term planning. Who do you think should get fired?

Woman: All the way to the top leaders. They are responsible for those under them. They should have set the standards and had more oversight.

Me: Homeland Security is a Cabinet Department, directly under the President.

Woman: Really? I didn't know that.

Me: Yes. President Truman had a sign on his desk that said, "The buck stops here," because he was opposed to the idea of passing the buck when there was a problem. We could probably use more of that mentality these days.

Woman: I agree.... I didn't know the President was directly over the agency hurting those kids. I'll have to think about that some more... Maybe do some research...

Me: That's always a good idea.

Muslim: You shouldn't be supporting gay people as a Muslim.

Me: Muslims are supposed to protect the oppressed. If you don't think the LGBTQ community is oppressed, that's a major problem. By the way, what are you doing to support oppressed Black people in the US?

Muslim: We don't have any power other than prayer.

Me: Prayer should move you to action and love for your fellow humans, not resignation and judgment.

Woman: Why do you push so hard on gay issues?

Me: Because it's a major issue that crosses many demographics.

Woman: But it's a sin.

Me: So is judging others. More importantly, no one's asking you to be gay or even to approve of them. They're demanding that everyone stay out of their personal lives, and especially their bedrooms. Surely, we all want to preserve that freedom. I know I do.

Woman: Women getting abortions paid for by the government is wrong!

Me: Which are you against, abortion or the government paying for it?

Woman: The government paying for it!

Me: Then there is no problem because the government isn't paying for it.

Woman: I read they do!

Me: Only in cases of incest or rape or if the life of the mother is in danger. And only then for those already poor.

Woman: So, all they have to do is lie and say they were raped or molested!

Me: That could actually be a problem if we limit abortion to only those who are raped or molested. Unfortunately, rape and incest are already a big enough real problem now that focusing on THAT should be a higher priority than taking even more power away from women over their own bodies.

Woman: We already have a criminal justice system that deals with that.

Me: Like Brock Turner, who dragged an unconscious woman behind a dumpster to rape her and only served three months? Not much of a deterrent… and zero justice.

Woman: That's an exception.

Me: So is the government paying for abortion.

Man: I'll check you out. If I like what I see, I'll sign your petition online.

Me: Great! Here's my social media card with all the places you can find my stances, including the most detailed website of any US Senate candidate.

Man: What's your stance on National Security?

Me: We need to stop militarily intervening in international conflicts that don't serve or protect us.

Man: That's a vague answer.

Me: It's not meant to be. What are we talking about? Domestic national security? Terrorism? Syria bombing?

Man: The military budget. It's out of control.

Me: We can reduce the military budget by focusing on protecting our country instead of being militarily involved in international nation-building. I signed a contract to push for raising the education budget every time we raise the military budget. If we're going to invest in training to kill people and destroy things, we also need to invest in training to heal people and build our country. All that and more is on my website.

Man: Give me your petition.

Reporter: If you were in the Senate right now, what legislation would you write?

Me: One issue. One paragraph. "The United States of America doesn't put children in cages, ever."

Finding Humor

I can find humor in intense situations because I know none of it is personal.

Even when others try to make it personal, it's rarely about me. Or you, as the case may be.

This is when knowing your triggers is most helpful. It's hard to find humor when someone hits your hot button.

The question to ask is, why is it your hot button?

It's often because it's a value your hold dear, a characteristic you take pride in having, or a previous injury.

Think about the topics that "set you off." Not big issues like world hunger or homelessness. We're talking about someone who questions your integrity, your faith, your looks, etc.

You will know a trigger because it's the topic that makes you lose all focus, causes you physical pain when you hear it, that heat rising from your abdomen that can actually make you shake in anger.

Figure out why it's a trigger. Then work on coming to terms with it.

Until you analyze and face your triggers, the best answer is often to exit a conversation when you hear a trigger – but you can't even figure out when to look for an exit strategy if you don't recognize it's your Achilles heel first.

And some triggers aren't because you have a problem with them but because you get tired of having to respond to the same comment over and over.

Examples would be height (tall or short) or that, as a woman, you should smile more.

Coming up with a humorous response can help you respond without getting stuck in the exasperation of it all.

If it's not personal, if it's not a trigger, if it's not true about you, much humor can be found.

Much like imagining everyone is naked while giving a speech to calm your nerves, seeing the ridiculousness of a comment or taking the words literally can open up endless possibilities for humor.

Protestor: I wish I had some bacon to rub all over your face!

Me: You understand bacon is not garlic, and I'm not a vampire, right?

Protestor: But it would condemn you to hell!

Me: Nope. But it would likely land you in jail.

Protestor: Bill Clinton slept with so many women! He was a predator!

Me: Hi! I'm Deedra Abboud, running for US Senate for Arizona.

Protestor: I know who you are!

Me: I wasn't sure since you were asking me about someone else's husband.

Protestor: You're from Arkansas, and I bet you voted for Hillary!

Me: Guilt by association?

Protestor: Is it true?!

Me: That I'm from Arkansas? Yes. That I voted for Hillary? Yes. That Bill is not my husband? Yes. That we're in 2018? Yes.

Woman: Where are you from?

Me: Arkansas.

Woman: When did you move to Arkansas?

Me: About nine months before I was born.

Woman: I don't think I've seen you in red before.

Me: I'm wearing #RedForEd

Woman: Who's Ed?

Me: Every child in Arizona who is missing out on educational opportunities because we keep defunding education and underpaying teachers...

Woman: Oh....

Me: No, really, it's a hashtag about fixing the problem of Arizona being the bottom of the barrel in education. We wear red every Wednesday to bring attention to it and put pressure on state legislators to address it.

Woman: Oh. Should I start wearing red on Wednesdays?

Me: We'd love for you to do that! The more people involved and showing support, the better.

Woman: I love everything about you and your platform, but I just have one problem with you.

Me: What is it?

Woman: Your scarf.

Me: You have a problem with a piece of my clothing?

Woman: Yes. It's a symbol of oppression.

Me: Not to me.

Woman: It is. Your religion forces you to wear it.

Me: Actually, it doesn't. Religion doesn't force you to do anything. People pick and choose what religion says all the time.

Woman: I have a real problem with it. It upsets me to see you wear it.

Me: Would it help if I wore it differently? What if I kept it on my head but not on my shoulders, more like the African style?

Woman: Yes. I think I could handle that. I think that would be better.

Me: So, you think you have a right to decide how I dress?

Woman: No. You can dress however you want. I'm just not sure I can vote for you if you wear the scarf like that.

Me: So, you need me to get undressed so you can vote for me?

Woman: You need to know that a man makes you wear that on your head.

Me: What man?

Woman: The Middle East.

Me: I'm not from the Middle East. I'm from Arkansas.

Woman: I know, but American women don't wear that.

Me: What about nuns, Mennonites...

Woman: That's different.

Me: After 9/11, my husband told me I could take it off. I told him I didn't put it on for him, and I don't need his permission to take it off.

Woman: In America, women don't wear that!

Me: I believe women should be able to dress however they want and the only person whose business it is... is the woman looking back at her in the mirror. I will fight for that right for all women.

Woman: Men love it when you wear that!

Me: Men love it when we wear bikinis, so should we stop wearing those?

Woman: Women love it when men wear Speedos!

Me: I don't know about that!

[We both laugh]

Woman: Anyway, I love that you're running. Keep it up!

Woman: I have problems with the headscarf. Just as I have with any female head covering or female dress, based on the belief that women must control their behavior and dress because of men. Your religion does not bother me; the message you send does. I will always have a problem with that.

Me: The fact that I don't wear the scarf for men doesn't matter?

Woman: You don't understand what the scarf means. It's a form of oppression.

Me: How do you feel about transgender women?

Woman: What does that have to do with anything?

Me: I was just wondering if you also feel you have the right to determine how all women show up across the board or if it's just Muslim women.

Woman: People who want to be a different gender doesn't affect my life.

Me: Neither do my clothing choices. But you deciding you have the right to decide what I believe and how I can dress does affect my freedom.

Man [as he's walking by]: U.S. Senate, huh. You know you're swimming upstream, right?

Me [start walking beside him]: You know salmon do that every year successfully, right?

[shocked stare, walks away slowly]

Me: One of the major issues on the First Nation lands is lack of access to cell and Internet services.

Woman: I would think that their culture and traditions would mean they don't care about the Internet and cell phones.

Me: How do you think they communicate? Smoke signals? Just because they want to keep their traditions doesn't mean they reject modern technology.

Protestor: You have a 100-year plan to take over the United States. I've read it!

Me: I didn't get the memo. But it's interesting that you got the memo you say was meant for me. Was it addressed to me?

Woman: How do you handle all the crazy comments and questions you get?

Me: What's the alternative? Being an ostrich is over-rated.

It Is What It Is

Sometimes conversations just "are."

There's no point.

No disagreement.

No epiphanies.

Maybe it's just listening, or the exchange of information that may or may not be useful.

Or maybe it's just surviving the moment or situation.

It's all okay.

At a community support event after the Tempe Mosque vandalism:

Woman: Wow! I didn't realize there were so many Muslims who aren't Arab.

Me: Yes, Arabs are less than 20% of the 1.8 billion Muslims in the world.

Woman: And look at all the white ones. I had no idea. And look...so many Asians too!

Me: Yes, and 40% of American-born Muslims are Black. Boggles the mind, doesn't it?

Woman: Yes. It does....

A video of this event can be found on YouTube – Deedra2018: "Deedra at Love and Coffee."

A related video of the woman who vandalized the Tempe Mosque can also be found on YouTube – Deedra2018: "Love is more powerful than Hate on Phoenix streets."

Woman: Can I give you some constructive criticism?

Me: Always.

Woman: I attended the Love & Coffee event after that girl attacked you and the Mosque. Everyone talked about standing with and including Native Americans, People of Color, the LGBTQ community. All of the minority groups. But not one speaker mentioned standing with the disability community. It's like that at every single event.

Me: Agreed. Noted. I will strive to do better.

Woman: Are you going to March For Our Lives this weekend?

Me: I'm going to the Sierra Vista one!

Woman: Why would you do that? There will be so many more people in Phoenix.

Me: I got invited to #MarchForOurLives Phoenix, Tucson, Sierra Vista, and Kingman. I asked myself, "Which march will be least likely to have a federal candidate or official join them?" And I chose Sierra Vista. I'll have some campaign volunteers at Phoenix, though!

A funny related story: A woman started telling people I lost her vote because she saw me sit on the edge of the stage at the Phoenix #MarchForOurLives event, taking space that should have been reserved for those with disabilities.

Many people responded that I was not at the Phoenix event because I was at the Sierra Vista event… 188 miles, 3 hours away.

She saw a woman wearing a scarf and assumed it was me.

It started a whole joke that all scarf-wearing women in Arizona must be Deedra.

Man: These events must get really tiring... having to meet and talk to all kinds of people every single day.

Me: Not to me. I love it! But I can see where it would get tiring for people with the intention of just coming in and shaking as many hands as possible so they can leave.

Man: So, what's your intention when you come to these events?

Me: To meet whoever I'm supposed to meet and make connections with whoever I'm supposed to make connections with.

Man: Wow! I really like that!

While talking to a small group, I notice a man enter the room and stand near us.

Me [turning to him]: *Hi! I'm Deedra.*

Man: I know. I was leaving another event and recognized you through the door in this room. I just wanted to meet you and tell you I support you.

Me: *Thank you! It's a pleasure to meet you!*

Man: I'm an Independent and just love your campaign. I live on the west side, and I'm telling people about you every chance I get!

Me: *That's great! Do you have all my social media?*

Man: I've been following your campaign on Facebook.

Me: *We've got a lot more than that. We're even on YouTube! Take a social media card! Take several...and share them!*

Man: Will do! I absolutely wish you the best of luck and can't wait to vote for you!

Woman: I'm Independent, so I can't vote in the primary. But good luck!

Me: I've got good news! I didn't save a bunch of money on car insurance, BUT Independents CAN vote in Arizona primaries, just not the Presidential ones.

Woman: Really? I didn't know that. I was turned away when I tried to vote in the Presidential primary and just thought the law had changed or something!

Me: Nope. Now you know!

Woman: Thank you for telling me. Now I can vote for you!

Me: My pleasure. For both!

Woman: Will I see you at the #MarchForOurLives tomorrow?

Me: No. I'll be in Sierra Vista at their march. You're going?

Woman: Yes!

Me: So, you're into politics now?

Woman: Oh, no. But my daughter is a volunteer at the event, and I have never seen her so motivated and organized. She's finding out she's a leader! I'm loving it!

Me: That's fantastic!

Woman: I keep seeing you post #RedForEd on Facebook. Who's Ed?

Me: Are you making a joke about my #CampaignChronicles, or you're really asking who Ed is?

Woman: I'm really asking.

Me: Ok. Ed stands for education. #RedForEd is about wearing red to raise awareness for the systematic and deliberate defunding of education in Arizona that is hurting our children and our economy. I posted a #CampaignChronicle about a lady asking the same question.

Woman: Oh. I must have missed that chronicle.

Woman: We all came together for Prop 206 and got our living wage. It worked!

Me: Yes. It's called collective bargaining. It's what Unions do. Imagine what would happen if we supported them.

Man: All I want to know is your position on cannabis.

Me: It's on my website. Total transparency. It needs to be decriminalized on the federal level and let states decide from there.

Man: Give me your petition.

Man: Will you be having US Senate candidate debates or forums?

Me: That's the most common question I have gotten since January. Several groups have told me they've been trying, with no success.

Man: Are you willing to do it?

Me: Absolutely! It should be standard for primary and general elections on all levels.

Woman: I don't vote because my vote doesn't matter. I voted to legalize cannabis last election, and it lost.

Me: Voting isn't just about winning what you want. It's about progress. On cannabis, for example, if 20% vote for it and it loses, politicians think people don't care about it. If 40% vote for it, and it loses, politicians realize it is an important issue to voters. That's how we make our voices heard and move the conversations even when we don't get exactly what we want instantly.

Woman [eyes light up]: Oh. Wow! I never thought of it that way.

Woman: I don't think I've ever seen you in red.

Me: I'm wearing #RedForEd. It's a problem because I only have one red outfit.

Woman: I thought that was last week?

Me: It's every Wednesday, so we don't let them forget.

Walking around a community fair:

Woman [in a booth]: Hey! Come here!

[I walk over to her]

Woman: Tell me why you're dressed that way.

Me: This is how I dress.

Woman [sees my name tag]: Oh! You're running for office! That's why. You look amazing. Your jacket... your pants... your boots... your rainbow umbrella. Just amazing!

Me: Thanks!

Woman: You have a petition to sign?

Me: Yes. [hand her petition]

Woman: I love how you're so put together. Just keep doing what you're doing!

At Phoenix Pride festival:

Woman: What's your sexual orientation? Am I allowed to ask that?

Me: You can ask anything. I'm straight.

Woman: So, you're heterosexual?

Me: Yes.

Woman: Are you married?

Me: Yes.

Woman: Do you have kids?

Me: No.

Woman: I'll sign your petition!

Me: Thanks! Check out the social media too. It's hot!

Woman: I think you could really win.

Me: That's the plan.

Woman: I'm so embarrassed to tell you that I sent you a message when you first announced that there was no way you could win, but it was probably a good thing you were running so people could get used to the idea of a Muslim in our society. I really am sorry I said that. You have earned my vote.

Me: Thank you.

Her husband: I've been a supporter since day one. Thank you for running!

Boy [9 years old]: Can my mom vote twice for you?

Me: No. Everyone only gets one vote.

Boy: What if someone forgets to vote and you're one short?

Me: That's why it's so important that we remind everyone to vote from now. We can't afford anyone to forget.

Boy: I wish I was 18 so I could vote for you.

Me: Me too!

Boy: Can I remind people who are 18 to vote even though I can't vote?

Me: Yes, you can. And people will love that!

IT IS WHAT IT IS

At a RAVE:

Man [20's, Muslim]: What are you doing here?

Me: Getting people registered to vote and talking about how we can change the political landscape in Arizona!

Man: No. What are you doing _here_?

Me: Cause this is where you are.

Man: You know you're at a RAVE, right?

Me: It was hard to miss with the costumes & five bands that I'm trying to talk over. I didn't just happen by. The organizers invited me.

Man: Wow! That's like so cool! [sees my name tag] You're running for office? I never met anybody running for office before! It's so cool you're here! Thanks!

Woman: I wear my Deedra2018 button around Yuma, and so many people get excited when they see it. They say they're already following you and love your campaign. Most of them are under 30.

Me: Thanks so much for sporting our swag! Swag is a powerful tool. Here are some social media cards so you can spread the word to even more people!

Woman: I would love to! Thanks so much for being the kind of leader we need now!

IT IS WHAT IT IS

Man 1: I'm an Independent.

Man 2: And I'm a Republican.

Man 1: We came here [event] looking for options.

Man 2: And we both agree you are our option.

Me: Great! I'll keep earning your vote! Did ya'll come together?

Man 1: No. We just met tonight. Why?

Me: It was like y'all were talking in unison.

Man 2: Well, I think we'll start being friends now.

[We all laugh]

Me: I love that! I'm glad I could help bring y'all together! United We Rise, you know!

[We all laugh]

Man [border patrol checkpoint officer]: How are you ladies doing?

Me: Excellent! How about you?

Man: I'm good. [trying to look in my backseat]

[I roll down window]

Me: That's all campaign stuff in the back.

Man: Ya. I've been seeing a lot of your friends come through. [talking about other candidates and volunteers leaving event]

Me: I'm Deedra. I'm running for US Senate. Flake's seat.

Man: Oh ya! One of your volunteers came by a while ago. He told me all about you.

Me & Tara [in unison]: Nathan?

Man: Ya! Nathan. He was really excited about your campaign, told me all about you, and gave me some campaign cards. Good luck!

Talking to a woman running for office at a public event, really connecting.

Me: I also use my social media to promote down-ballot. It's so important that we all work together and let people know they have options all over the ballot this year.

Woman: I love that! I'll be promoting you too. I love your platform and your social media!

[Woman walks away. I turn to Tara.]

Me: I can't believe I don't recognize her name. I've made it a point to know every single candidate running on the state and federal level. When I get home, I'll have to check my spreadsheet. I can't believe I missed a candidate.

Tara: She's Republican.

Me: Oh. Well, that's exciting since we got along so well. I wonder if she was confused about my party, too?

Man: You don't have kids?

Me: No.

Man: They're going to go after you on family values.

Me: If they do, it will be an equalizing attack. Neither of my opponents has kids that I know of. And I'm the only one married.

IT IS WHAT IT IS

Man: Do you have kids?

Me: No.

Man: That's going to be a problem.

Me: Funny. Women with children usually hear that it's a problem.

Man: We're in Arizona. Wouldn't it be better if you just said you support the Second Amendment with zero restrictions?

Me: So, you're suggesting that I lie and then do whatever I want once I'm elected?

Man: Well... yes.

Me: Isn't that how we got into the mess we're in?

IT IS WHAT IT IS

Woman 1: I'm concerned about the silent majority of racists in America.

Woman 2: They're not silent.

Me: They're not the majority.

Nature of the Beast

Part of my value of honesty revolves around root causes. It's not always what people say but what it means.

That's not to say I assume what people mean. I don't. I believe in taking what people say at face value.

However, I do focus on exactly what they say means: The consequences or possible outcome.

And that's what I focus on in my response.

Often, what came out of their mouth is not what they meant, and I give them the opportunity to rephrase or explain by repeating what I believe I heard them say.

Sometimes, they were only focused on the immediate outcome and will backtrack once the long-term, often unintended, consequences are pointed out to them.

Other times I just remain quiet, so the silence offers them the opportunity to hear what they said and reflect on what it sounded like.

Most people aren't comfortable with silence.

But it is a powerful tool because most people will feel the need to explain if they don't get immediate feedback.

Questions are also powerful.

The further explanations are the real meat to find out where they're coming from, where they're meaning to go, and what the real issue is.

Woman: You're married?

Me: Yes. 18 years.

Woman: Do you have kids?

Me: No.

Woman: That's going to be a problem as a candidate.

Me: Why?

Woman: Family values.

Me: So, a person without children can't have family values?

Woman: No... I mean... Well, a lot of people won't think you can really care about children if you never had them.

Me: [just smile]

Woman: Oh! I didn't mean to offend you!

Me: You didn't offend me. I'm giving you time to hear what you just said.

Woman: Arizona is a conservative state. We can't win running on Democratic values. We have to compromise.

Me: Is a living wage a progressive value?

Woman: Yes.

Me: Arizonans passed a living wage initiative in 2016, despite huge money opposition. The same can be said about passing medical cannabis. Maybe not running on our values is the real problem.

Man: As Democrats, we need to stick to demanding access to affordable healthcare for everyone.

Me: What does access to affordable healthcare for everyone mean?

Man: It means everyone can get healthcare because it is affordable.

Me: Affordable to whom? How? Will we stop the health insurance companies from price gouging? Will we stop the malpractice insurance companies from just settling suits and raising the rates on doctors? Will we look at standardizing pricing on some level? Will we demand pharmaceutical companies negotiate prices?

Man: We don't have the details. Once Democrats take over the House and Senate, then they can write the bills and debate them.

Me: Those of us fighting for Medicare for All already have bills discussing these things. We're not asking you to just trust us.

Woman: People didn't get out and vote, even with all that's going on in the world. There's just no reaching them.

Me: Primaries always have a low turnout for a lot of reasons. But this year had a record turnout. That's progress. Midterms have a higher turnout than primaries but a lower turnout during the presidential years. We've got a lot going for us this November, but it will all be wasted if we keep leading with our own defeatism.

Woman: But we can't change the minds of the Trumpsters!

Me: I agree, and I'm not sure why we keep focusing on that 33% when everyone else is hungry for something to vote FOR. They're literally walking around living their own lives waiting for you to give them the good news about a candidate that they can believe in.

Woman: I just don't know what to do anymore.

Me: Are you interested in any candidate or initiative?

Woman: I don't know anything about any of them.

Me: Not even Save Our Schools or #RedForEd?

Woman: Oh yes! I'm really passionate about public education! But I heard the initiative is off the ballot.

Me: The Invest in Ed is off the ballot, but No on 305, the SOS initiative, is still going strong. Why don't you start there? Start making sure everyone you know also knows to vote No on 305? Maybe volunteer for Save Our Schools? Maybe go to some of the local candidate forums or legislative district meetings so you can learn more about candidates on all levels. Maybe one of these things will be that spark you need so you can see all the amazing things happening, all the amazing people working their butts off, instead of just what's not happening.

Muslim: I don't vote because all government is corrupt.

Me: Voting is how you change things with your hand and your tongue. Hating it in your heart is supposed to be your last choice, not your first one.

Woman: The government forcing businesses not to discriminate takes away our freedoms. Like, I would support a baker for refusing to bake a cake for a 10-year-old child bride wedding!

Me: Discrimination laws only apply to protected classes. Refusing service to people for any characteristic or trait that is not part of protected class status is completely legal. You can, for example, legally discriminate against child bride marriages, or even blue-eyed people, all day. Under several states' current laws, transgender isn't a protected class either, despite advances we've made with LGBTQ protection laws.

Woman: We need to help people in [x] country.

Me: If we can't protect our rights in our own country, if we can't even depend on the rule of law lately, what do you think we can do for people in other countries?

Woman: We're still okay. Their needs are bigger. Some of them are dying, and there's so much oppression.

Me: Our children are in fear for their lives going to school, and if we continue to privatize education, they might not be able to go anyway. Immigrant children are scared their parents will disappear before they get home from school. Calling the police for simple matters is putting people's lives in danger. Flint still doesn't have clean water, and Puerto Rico's infrastructure is still like a third world country. People are literally dying because they can't afford healthcare. You might be doing okay, but maybe you should start checking on your neighbors.

Woman: I'm conservative, but I'm liberal on social issues:

Me: What does that mean?

Woman: I'm liberal on social inclusion and social programs, but I am conservative on spending money.

Me: You mean you want money spent on social programs but don't want money wasted?

Woman: Yes.

Me: The idea of fiscally conservative has come to mean cheap... starving the social programs to death. What it should mean is economical... spend money wisely for the social benefit.

Woman: Yes! I want us to be economical!

Me: So do Democrats. None of us want to waste money, and starving social programs hurts everybody. All of us want to be more economical.

Woman: So, I'm not fiscally conservative?

Me: Not according to the current term usage. How about we drop the short-cut labels and start defining what we mean?

Woman: I like that!

Woman: Did you hear about the Walgreen's pharmacist refusing to fill the lady's prescription due to his strongly held religious belief?

Me: Yes. Yet another attack on women's sexual freedom.

Woman: This doesn't have anything to do with women's sexual freedom! This was about a pharmacist interfering with her healthcare!

Me: First, they stopped schools from teaching girls how to prevent venereal diseases and pregnancy. Then they attacked abortion, not head-on but in a paper-cut fashion. Then they attacked Planned Parenthood, which prevented lots of people from having any kind of healthcare but particularly around sexual activity. Then they attacked women's access to birth control through their insurance companies if their employer wanted a say. Then pharmacists started refusing to fill the Morning-After pill prescriptions. Then they put a gag order on doctors giving their patients full details about their options when pregnant. It's all about women's sexual freedom. But too many people see these as separate issues instead of a steady path in one direction, complete control of women's freedom and sexual choices.

Man: Every other country deports illegals, in many cases imprisons, kills, or even tortures them. We're not doing anything worse.

Me: Which countries?

Man: I don't know. Lots of them. North Korea! Russia! Probably the Middle East too!

Me: We used to condemn those countries for their treatment of people. Now we use them to justify our behavior?

Man: That's not what I mean! I mean, at least we're not as bad as them.

Me: We used to strive to be the best in all things. Now we're scraping the bottom of the barrel to find anyone doing worse, so we feel better?

Man: We're showing strength and protecting OUR country.

Me: There are 195 countries in the world. The vast majority are looking at our actions in horror, many for the first time in history. The only ones cheering are the dictatorships we used to condemn.

Man: Healthcare for all is not reasonable.

Me: Why not? Every industrialized country in the world, including Capitalist countries, have figured it out. Why are we suddenly the country that can't? Not to mention it's listed on the DNC website as a Democratic value.

Man: It's just a Democratic aspiration. No realistic candidate is pushing for it.

Me: An aspiration is a goal that you work toward. If we're not working toward it, it's a lie, and people will die. In fact, they already are.

Man: Republicans and Independents don't want it. Democrats know that. That's why real candidates aren't talking about it.

Me: While I'm traveling around the state actually talking to real people, I am finding Republicans and Independents do want a healthcare system that works and doesn't bankrupt them for someone else's profit. The only thing they're worried about is paying more and getting less. Once I point out that that's what's already happening, we usually have good conversations about it.

Man: It's just not realistic.

Me: When I was young, I thought about going to law school, but I was poor and didn't see it as a real possibility. It wasn't an aspiration until I decided to work toward doing it. We can't call Healthcare for All an aspiration while we are actively working against ever getting it. That's not only self-defeating but dishonest.

Man: Would you support the Secure and Succeed Act?

Me: No. I don't believe in second-class citizenship. That bill would give some, not all, Dreamers a path to citizenship after a 12-year green card and give DACA recipients a path to citizenship after a 10-year green card... and neither would ever be able to sponsor a family member.

Man: It's better than nothing.

Me: It legally creates a second-class citizenship in the 21st century. Once that is established law, second-class citizenship for other groups becomes possible.

Man: The Supreme Court would rule second-class citizenship unconstitutional.

Me: Then why advocate for an unconstitutional law in the first place? And ruling the law unconstitutional would put all those who benefited right back into status uncertainty. That's just kicking the can down the road, not a solution.

Woman: How does the scarf make you feel?

Me: What do you mean?

Woman: Do you like it?

Me: I can't imagine choosing to wear something every day that I didn't like.

Woman: I just thought it might make people act negatively toward you.

Me: I have to deal with those people whether I'm running for office or not. At least now we can have the conversations about it.

Woman: Yes. I'm Jewish, but I don't wear the star because I don't want people to treat me bad.

Me: I'd like us to work on changing that feeling together. People should be able to wear whatever they want and be whatever they want without being harassed.

Woman: I know abortion will still happen when we outlaw it, but it will be less because it will be too dangerous to choose.

Me: We made that same argument when we decided to build the border wall along Mexico except in the extreme desert areas, claiming it would reduce illegal entry because people would be too scared to cross the desert. And if they died trying, that was okay too. As a deterrent.

Woman: We can't take away the tax breaks to corporations because that's how we bring businesses to Arizona.

Me: Yet despite the tax breaks, businesses are not choosing Arizona because we don't have an educated workforce they can depend on. Intel even said they would have located somewhere else had they known Arizona education would sink to the level we have. If we continue to give tax breaks without investing in education, the only types of businesses we will attract are those who don't care about the future of our state.

Woman: Haven't you learned yet you aren't going to change the minds of people filled with hate or lacking empathy for humanity? You're wasting your time.

Me: I've never tried to change anyone's mind about anything. By engaging in conversations and making strong statements of my values, I may be planting a seed, but more importantly, I'm proudly standing up against those ideas publicly for all to see. People need to see that. It's for the witnesses, not necessarily the person I'm talking to.

Man: What do you say to people who say you're not qualified for US Senate and should have run for a lower office first?

Me: As a woman, I've been told that for almost every job I've ever applied for. I've also met state legislators that didn't know the difference between an Arizona resident, a Permanent Resident, and a US citizen. So, having held office doesn't make one automatically qualified. I'm qualified because I'm an attorney, and I know how the government works. I know how to communicate with expertise in uncomfortable conversations. I know how to negotiate. I've been traveling all over Arizona listening to Arizonans for more than 15 years as well as during this campaign, and I've run a competitive campaign against a well-funded opponent.

Woman: I'm not into politics.

Me: Aren't you vegan?

Woman: Yes.

Me: Why?

Woman: Because all the killing and eating of animals is inhumane and is hurting our environment. And it's healthier not to eat meat.

Me: So, you care about the environment, treatment of animals, and health but have chosen not to be involved with decisions about them?

Woman: I don't eat meat, and I educate people about why they shouldn't either.

Me: That's good. I educate people about how their vote actually determines who makes the laws to help or hurt those things.

Woman: You're already gathering signatures but remember not to turn them in until just before their due.

Me: Why?

Woman: In the class I took, that's what they said.

Me: But you don't know why they said to do it?

Woman: No.

Me: It's a tactic. I can see some reasons for it, but without knowing why you're following the tactics, how can you know if it fits into your larger strategy?

Woman: I don't know. I just know it's a rule.

Me: There are no rules. There is only strategy. It's always good to know why you're doing something before you do it. Even when an expert tells you something, it's best to ask why – even when you think you can see the logic.

Man: We pay foreign aid because we have a responsibility to rebuild the countries we destroyed.

Me: We haven't paid direct reparations to rebuild countries we've destroyed since Germany and Japan. The largest recipients of US foreign aid are Afghanistan, Egypt... and Israel, who has Universal Healthcare while we don't. Most of it is for military assistance, so they can buy weapons from US companies.

Man: Oh. I guess I need to rethink how I understand our foreign aid.

Woman: Kim Davis had a right to refuse to give marriage licenses to gay couples because her religion is against gay marriage.

Me: Should a Hindu person have the right to refuse to give hunting licenses because killing animals is against his or her religion?

Woman: No. That's different.

Me: How about people do the jobs they were hired or elected to do and avoid jobs that interfere with their religious beliefs?

Not Taking the Bait

The most frequent tactic I faced as a political candidate was loaded first contact comments.

A person's initial engagement being an inflammatory topic.

Having conversations with strangers about controversial topics is the hardest to handle.

We don't know each other. We can't know where we're coming from, where we're meant to go, and there is zero trust.

And the intent is too often meant to antagonize or trigger rather than engage in a conversation that might find common ground.

Too often, the response is to focus on the "issue" from a defensive position.

I don't.

I recognize it as bait, and I choose not to take the bait.

Instead, I choose to take the conversation somewhere else.

While I'm not solving any world problems with this tactic, I'm preserving my peace of mind, not giving them any ammunition, and likely frustrating them.

Sometimes that's the best you can hope for when the original intent was never to connect or create a dialogue.

You can't control other people, but you can control your response to them.

Woman: Some women have lied about being raped.

Me: Some rapists have confessed to being rapists.

Woman: What does that have to do with anything?

Me: Nothing. I thought we were playing an exception to the rule game.

Protestor: I don't want Sharia in our government!!!

Me: Me either! Let's work together to keep all religions out of our government!

Man: You hate Jews!

Me: Nope!

Man: Yes, you do! All Muslims hate Jews!

Me: Nope! ALL Muslims don't anything.

Man: I've never met a Muslim who didn't hate Jews!

Me: Now you have. I can even introduce you to some Muslims happily married to Jews.

Man: It's all over the Internet that you hate Jews.

Me: It's all over the Internet that we never landed on the moon. That's not true either.

Man: You've made statements that you hate Jews.

Me: Nope. Not in 46 years of my life have I made such a statement. Not publicly, nor privately. Because it's not true.

Man: I know you hate Jews!

Me: I know I don't.

Man: You will never convince me that you don't hate Jews!

Me: On that, I might have to agree with you.

Man: [turns and storms off]

Protestor: You say you support LGBTQ rights, but your religion says to throw them off buildings.

Me: Nope.

Protestor: Yes. That's what you believe.

Me: Nope. But it's funny that you're gonna tell me what I believe.

Protestor: Your religion says to throw them off buildings! How can you believe that?!

Me: I don't. Nor does my religion. That's ISIS, who are terrorists killing everybody, including Muslims. They don't represent me or talk for me.

Protestor: No! Your religion says to throw them off buildings.

Me: Where in the Quran does it say that?

Protestor: It's in there!

Me: 1,400 years ago, they didn't have buildings, so where in the Quran does it say that?

Man: Somebody told me you want to kill gays.

Me: Somebody told you wrong.

Man: But your religion says you have to kill them.

Me: Nope. In fact, I've known my aunt is gay my entire life. That's 46 years. She's still gay. She's still my aunt. I still love her. And she's still alive. So, there's that.

Man: You're not fit for political office because you don't believe in gender equality! You have to be subservient to Arab men, your masters!

Me: 80% of Muslims aren't Arab.

Man: You know your religion requires you to obey men!

Me: Nope. Look at me standing up to you now.

Man: I mean Muslim men!

Me: I'm fairly certain religion doesn't change your gender. You're describing culture, not religion. American culture has a sexist element too, and I reject that as well.

Muslim: Why don't you speak Arabic?

Me: I understand a lot of it if I concentrate on the conversation, but I can't think of the words to reply fast enough.

Muslim: You've been Muslim how long?

Me: 19 years.

Muslim: And you're married to an Arab?

Me: Yes, for 18 years.

Muslim: Then you should have learned it by now.

Me: I became Muslim, not Arab.

Woman*: You're a brave woman.

Me: Why?

Woman: You just walked up in here, not scared of nothin'. All by yourself, dressed like you are, and a Democrat.

Me: You think I should have something to fear from you or others?

Woman: No. We're nice people. But I would think you would be scared.

Me: I don't live in fear. But does it not concern you that you think I would be afraid of walking around freely in my own country?

Woman: I don't know. I guess it's just the times we live in.

Me: It doesn't have to be. Each of us chooses how to show up with each other, and we choose whether to hold our social groups accountable for bad behavior. Some things are within our control.

*Border 'security' advocate, at an event where I was the only Democrat.

Man: I bet you don't even have a US flag hanging in front of your house!

Me: No one else in my neighborhood does either. I have both a US and Arizona flag in my car at all times for events, complete with 10-foot poles and stands. Does that count?

Woman: The parents shouldn't have brought their kids here, then they wouldn't be separated.

Me: We're keeping the kids, so what are we going to do with them?

Woman: What do you mean? They're in facilities to keep them safe.

Me: We're not returning them to the parents, so what are we doing with them?

Woman: I guess we'll put them in foster care.

Me: So, we the taxpayers are gonna pay for foster parents to raise them?

Woman: Wait. What? I hadn't thought of that. No! I don't want to pay for them to stay here!

Me: Maybe we should have thought of that before we started stealing people's kids.

Reporter: It must be hard to hear this [anti-Muslim] stuff since you announced?

Me: I was hearing it before. The only difference is now you know about it.

Man: I know people really like you, but we have to be practical this year. Expertise should outweigh charisma.

Me: What expertise are you looking for?

Man: Understanding the law. Understanding how the political system works. Being able to reach across the aisle and talk to people who don't agree with you. Ability to compromise.

Me: I'm an attorney, so I think law and compromise are within my wheelhouse. I've been a civil rights and social justice advocate for 15 years in Arizona, holding politicians accountable, so I'm fairly confident in my understanding of how our political system has worked and should work. I've stood up to the face of hate on Main Street and de-escalated conversations with White Nationalists. I have the expertise; the charisma is just a bonus.

Reporter: You think people should have hope?

Me: What's the alternative? [long pause] We can't solve all the problems in the world, but we can each do something. It's small bites. How do you eat an elephant? One bite at a time.

Outside Their Expectations

Similar to not taking the bait is responding outside their expectations.

Taking the conversation in a completely different direction than they intended or expected.

Since their intent is not to truly engage or find common ground in the first place, you don't owe them that either.

Sometimes, leaving people confused about you or the issue is the best gift you can give.

You've given them the opportunity to reflect later on.

Whether they do or not is on them.

I'm a seed planter, nothing more.

I'm not responsible for the rain or sunshine or whether something grows, only planting the seed.

Woman: The government doesn't give money to Meals-on-Wheels!

Me: Yes, they do.

Woman: No, they don't! I researched it! Meals-On-Wheels gets grants!

Me: Grants are the only way the government gives money to non-profits.

Woman: Oh.

Me: Other than that, are you against the government making sure the elderly and the disabled have food?

Woman: No one helped me when I was poor!

Me: How did that make you feel?

Woman: Like I needed to work harder!

Me: So, you want people literally homebound due to age or physical ailment to work for food?

Woman: Where are you from?

Me: Arkansas.

Woman: Where before that?

Me: I was born in Arkansas.

Woman: Where were your parents from?

Me: Arkansas and Oklahoma.

Woman: Oh, so you married an Arab.

Me: Yes, I did. But I became Muslim before I met him, and I converted him.

[lady looks confused]

Me: He was born Muslim but didn't know anything about Islam. I had to teach him. He was an excellent student, though!

Woman: I don't understand why they don't just come here legally.

Me: Most do.

Woman: No, I mean the illegal ones.

Me: So do I.

Woman: They can't have come here legally if they're illegal.

Me: That's exactly how it happens. People come here legally but they often can't renew or change their status once here. So, they're stuck... and usually rooted or desperate by that point.

Woman: That doesn't make any sense....

Me: I totally agree with you. Immigration is a mess. Becoming undocumented is super easy. Becoming documented is hard.

Woman: What do you think about small government?

Me: I don't want it small enough to fit in my bedroom. I do want it to be more efficient, though.

Man: How do you feel about the military?

Me: My stepdad was in the Vietnam War. My niece and nephew are Veterans of the Iraq war. My nephew is still in the military.

Man: So, how would you support them?

Me: Two things. Number one: We must support the soldiers when they return from missions. The VA and other medical care, as well as help in housing and jobs. Number two: We must support them when we deploy them by having set goals for missions and listening to the experts on the ground about what will and will not work. Too many missions fail, and too many soldiers are injured or die because we aren't listing to the experts on the ground who know better.

Man: I love you right now! I have a son in the military. I'll definitely sign your petition!

Man: What do you think about immigration?

Me: It depends on what part of immigration you are talking about. I believe we can regulate who we allow into our country and still retain our humanity.

Man: Illegals are bringing in drugs, even to the Navajo lands. It's even worse where you are in Phoenix.

Me: We were told criminals would be targeted, but that's not what we're seeing. What we're seeing is individual family members being deported. Men and women who are hardworking have their own small businesses and families, doing nothing wrong since their original immigration violation. Even when they have American spouses. Even when they have American children. Even when they have served our country as Veterans.

Man: Yes, that's what we're seeing. That's not what we wanted. We wanted the criminals kicked out.

Me: Immigration is complicated but losing our humanity is dangerous for all our futures.

Man: I heard Arpaio say that we should have Dreamers go back to their home countries for 6 months, work there, learn the cultures of their birthplace, be good US ambassadors, and earn their return for a Green Card. A lot like Mormon missionaries and the Peace Corps do. It's not Amnesty and gets them a status quickly. I think it's a good idea. What do you think?

Me: Is it an actual program with support like the Peace Corps and Mormon missionaries have, or will we just be dumping them in a foreign country for 6 months?

Man: I don't know. But I think they're smart kids; most have degrees, so they can figure it out for 6 months.

Me: I doubt you or I could figure it out in a foreign country in 6 months with no support. What if they don't speak the language? What if the country is one of the ones people are fleeing from now? What if they don't have any family there? Do we have a responsibility if we send them back and they are murdered? Are they guaranteed a return, or are there additional requirements for that Green Card?

Man: I don't know. That's a lot of questions.

Me: They're called unintended consequences and should always be a factor when considering solutions.

Woman: I don't mean anything bad, but I look around this meeting and just see older people. How are we going to reach the younger people and get them to vote?

Me: Not by expecting them to come to us and our meetings. They see that as boring. Too much like school. We have to go to them and meet them as equals.

Woman: Oh. Are you doing that?

Me: Sure! I go to RAVES and anywhere else I can find them. And I don't just focus on convincing them to vote. I actually have real conversations with them.

Man: What makes you different than your opponent?

Me: I'm here talking to you.

Woman: Our education system is worthless. Young people working as cashiers can't even give change without the computer telling them how much.

Me: Have you ever asked those cashiers where they went to school?

Woman: No. But you know it was a public school. Otherwise, they wouldn't be working as a cashier.

Me: So, you think defunding public schools is the answer?

Woman: Yes. Businesses will do a better job of educating our kids than the government.

Me: Businesses are focused on profit. Education is focused on educating. If businesses were so good at educating, they would teach their employees how to properly perform their job functions... like giving change.

Man [Navajo]: The US government was founded on Christianity.

Me: What commandments are included in the law?

Man: Thou shalt not kill.

Me: Thou shalt not steal, too. But not the other eight. You can covet your neighbor's wife and dishonor thy father all day, legally. Every country in the world also criminalizes theft and murder, even non-Christian countries. We didn't even have "In God We Trust" until the 1950s, way after our founding.

Man: But the founders were Christian.

Me: Correct me if I'm wrong, but weren't the Navajo here before the colonists? And I'm fairly certain the Navajo weren't Christian before the US government forced their children into "Indian Schools" for indoctrination.

Man: Yes. That's true. But we're Christian now.

Me: And that choice is a beautiful thing, but it should be a choice in a 21st Century civilized society, not law.

Man: Why do you talk about white supremacists?

Me: My mom worked the Timothy McVey case. I grew up knowing that white supremacists still existed in this country. I grew up learning about what they thought and believed. But they were a fringe group, social outcasts. Now their ideas are becoming accepted in the American marketplace of ideas. We need to talk about that.

Man: But it's so controversial.

Me: White supremacy shouldn't be controversial in 2018. All racism, sexism, xenophobia, antisemitism, and hate of entire groups of people for their personal characteristics should be condemned by a modern society... especially in a diverse society like the U.S.

Man: But it's going to turn people off.

Me: It doesn't turn me off when people talk rationally about fighting terrorism because I don't support terrorist ideas. We should be able to talk rationally about threats to our country... and white supremacy is a threat.

Man: How do you think you're going fight white supremacy?

Me: I have a super-power. The white supremacists think I change my color when I change my clothes, so they'll never see me coming. I've got some privilege and I'm not afraid to use it!

OUTSIDE THEIR EXPECTATIONS

At a RAVE in downtown Phoenix:

Man [to young man walking by]: Are you a registered voter?

Young Man: No, man! I don't waste my time with politics. [goes on & on explaining something about the greater universe]

Me: What are you into?

Young Man: Music. I love music. I make music.

Me: Do you upload it to the Internet?

Young Man: Yes!

Me: Then you should be worried about Net Neutrality.

Young Man: Yes! I am. We have to stop them from ruining the Internet! It's about freedom!

Me: Ya, voting is how you do that. We need to vote for people that will protect that freedom.

Young Man: Wow! I never thought about it that way. Let me fill that paper out!

Man: How do we fight all the negative stuff? When they go low, we go high? Or what?

Me: I do believe when they go low, we go high...

Man: ...How? It's not working.

Me: I don't think we really understood what we go high means. It's not ignoring the bad stuff or being docile. It's facing it. With strength. In our power and passion. With CLASS!

Man: I don't see how that can be done.

Me: Ok. An example. The United States of America doesn't put kids in cages, ever. No one can argue with that. They will try, mind you. But to argue with it means you believe there is a justification for the United States of America putting kids in cages, something we would condemn any other country for. Now ask them to name the justification, a reason a country known as the beacon of freedom and hope could morally put children in cages.

Man: What good is that?

Me: We've found a middle ground and identified a problem that could be solved today. A simple bill. One sentence that changes everything. Then we can build on it for larger concepts around who we are as a country, how we treat those already legally seeking asylum, immigration reform, and even criminal justice reform.

Man: I keep hearing Democrats say no one will vote for you because you're Muslim.

Me: Do they mean Republicans, Independents, or Democrats?

Man: I don't know.

Me: We're already reaching Republicans and Independents, and many are reacting positively. But if it's Democrats that have a problem with a Muslim candidate, that's definitely a conversation we need to have.

Woman: You can't win in Arizona as a Muslim.

Me: So, you think Arizona is full of prejudiced people who are more interested in personal characteristics than character and policy?

Woman: Yes.

Me: Having traveled all over Arizona for the last 15 years, and especially over the last year, I haven't found that to be true.

Woman: But there are a lot of people like that in this state.

Me: I'm not denying that. People with real prejudices do exist here, and not always overt, but they are a minority even among Republicans... and they also won't vote for any Democrat, bi-sexual or otherwise. We need to stop focusing on the minority and start focusing on the majority who actually care about our family, friends, and neighbors as well as the future of our state and county.

Woman: But how do we reach them? How do we know who they are?

Me: By actually talking about the real issues we all face and what our future can look like if we work together. We spend too much time putting people in categories, assuming we know what they believe, instead of having real conversations and searching for all the things we have in common.

Don [fellow canvasser]: Hi! Is [female name] around?

Man: She's busy.

Me: Hi! I'm Deedra Abboud, and I'm running for US Senate in the upcoming August 28th Primary.

Man: Hello.

Don: We're Democrats and just wanted to drop this information off for [female name] about some candidates in the upcoming primary. Can I ask if you're Independent or Republican? [no male name on our list for house]

Man: I'm Republican. And I don't like what the Democrats are doing to this country! You all are just messing things up in Washington and everywhere else! [starts to close door]

Me: We love you, though!

Man [re-opens door]: I wasn't talking about you personally.

Me: And I didn't think you were. I just think we need more love in the world, to remember we're all neighbors, and we gotta solve problems together.

Man: Ya. That's true. I'll give my wife this stuff when she wakes up.

Me: Thanks so much! Have a great day!

Pursue or Desist

1st Rule of Conversations

Know when you're not having one.

2nd Rule of Conversations

Know when you're dealing with a person whose sole purpose in life is to:

a) Cut other people down to make themselves feel superior
b) Argue just to argue [troll, winning, moving the goal post]
c) "Win" without ethics

#WhatAboutism

#FakeOutrage

#FalseEquivalency

Don't invest or absorb.

You can walk away.

"OK..." with a smile.

Woman [wearing a TRUMP pin, looks at my name tag]: You're running for US Senate?

Me: Yes.

Woman: You don't have a chance.

Me: I don't believe you know anything about my campaign.

Woman: Have you ever held office?

Me: No.

Woman: Then, you don't have a chance.

Me: Trump never held office.

Woman: But he is a businessman and a billionaire.

Me: I'm a businesswoman, I've never filed for bankruptcy, and I'm an attorney.

Woman: I won't hold that against you. My husband's an attorney. You never ask a question you don't know the answer to.

Me: That only works in the courtroom, not real life, if you want to connect with people and serve people.

[woman keeps talking, I smile and no longer respond, she doesn't notice]

Woman: I haven't heard of you before. You need to get yourself in the media.

Me: I've been in the local papers, local television, CNN, MSNBC...

Woman: I only watch PBS.

Walking around a community fair.

Woman [in a Republican booth]: Hey! Come here. You're running for something?

Me [walking over to her]: Yes. U.S. Senate. Flake's seat.

Man: Democrat? Independent? What?

Me: Democrat.

Woman: Of course, she is. The rainbow umbrella gives it away. Only a Democrat would do that.

Woman [wearing a TRUMP Pin]: You're Muslim?

Me: Yes.

Woman: Are you gay?

Me: ....No....

Woman: This year's going to be interesting. Arpaio and Ward will divide the conservative vote. The people will have to decide between a Muslim, a bisexual, or a lesbian.

Me: I hadn't heard McSally is a lesbian.

Woman: Everyone thinks she is. She sure acts like one.

Me: Is that a problem?

Woman: Among the Republicans? Absolutely! But as long as she doesn't admit it, they'll probably just pretend it's not true.

Man: Why can't the Muslims all follow one teaching?

Me: We don't have a hierarchy. People interpret and follow the scholarly interpretations that they choose.

Man: Well, you should have a hierarchy like Christians, and then you wouldn't have all these different ideas.

Me: Protestants don't have a hierarchy either...

Man: Ya, but Catholics do. We follow the Pope.

Me: Do all Catholics agree?

Man: No. [laughs] We argue all the time about scripture. [laughs]

Me: .....

Customer 1 [reading event sign]: Deedra for US Senate and Kelly...?

Me: Kelly Fryer for Governor.

Cashier [pointing at me]: That's Deedra.

Customer 1 [turns to look at me]: Oh my God! [quickly turns back around] She's the worst!

Customer 2: What's that supposed to mean?

Me: Hi. I'm Deedra. I don't believe we've met. [extend my hand]

Customer 1: I know who you are! I heard you speak. I don't like you at all! [turns his body and face to pointedly avoid looking at me]

Me: We've met? Was it at the Scottsdale coffee shop event?

Customer 1 [still refusing to look at me]: I know you from tv.

Me: I don't know anyone from TV. I know people in real life.

[I smile at his wife, who appears mortified]

Customer 1: I saw you on FOX!

Me: That's good. And I'm going to be on FOX again this week. But I'm standing in front of you now. [with a big smile]

Customer 1 ignores me and walks around me to leave.

Cashier: If people don't have anything good to say, they shouldn't say anything.

Customer 2: Do you get that a lot?

Me: Nope. Never happened before, actually. Most people in Arizona want to connect when given the opportunity. Never even had close to that kind of experience, not even in Lake Havasu or Kingman.

Customer 2: Well, I'm sorry that happened.

Me: Don't worry about it. People like him, closed off and unhappy with themselves, are dinosaurs. We're changing things every day!

Woman: When our military is deployed, they are separated from their children too. Think about that before you start talking about foreign kids!

Me: But their kids aren't put in cages, and they know where their kids are. We honor our soldiers by upholding our values, not by losing our humanity. They see enough of that while deployed.

Protestor: Americans could have more if illegals weren't getting welfare!

Me: The undocumented are not eligible for welfare.

Protestor: Well, they're getting it! I know several people who are!

Me: Have you turned them in?

Protestor: No.

Me: You know people who are breaking the law, but you're not turning them in? Why not?

Protestor: Well, I don't know them. I just heard about them.

Me: Oh. Rumors. Yes, those are hard to stop.

Woman: I know what the problem is with the school shootings. It's all the bullying and leaving those kids out of the clicks. They get so hurt and decide to turn their anger on their fellow students.

Me: Haven't all of the school shootings been white boys?

Woman: The Parkland shooter was Latino.

Me: He had a Latino sounding name, but he was adopted... he considered himself completely anglo... he posted many racist comments against Jews, Blacks, and Immigrants.

Woman: But he was bullied.

Me: Why haven't minorities took up school shootings? They've been bullied for years.

Woman: Because minorities are used to it. It's a new experience for our kids. We need to teach the kids to be nicer and more inclusive.

Me: So, you're saying it's much harder to be a white boy today?

Woman: Yes! I have two sons. They are discriminated against constantly. Studies are showing it's harder for boys to get into college now unless they're a minority. I even read a study that most Americans want girls now instead of boys because girls have so much more opportunity.

Me: I have to tell you this has been the most fascinating conversation I believe I've ever had. Very little surprises me anymore, but I can honestly say you have accomplished that.

Woman: Good. You need to understand that our boys need help.

Me: I agree they need help. Maybe we can get bullied minorities to teach them coping skills for feeling powerless.

Woman: [blank look]

At a house party in Tucson:

Woman: I'm so excited to meet you! I hadn't heard of you. You really need to work harder to get your name out. I'm having a family picnic with a bunch of friends in Oro Valley after this event if you want to come.

Me: Sure. I'm free for a few hours and I gotta eat!

[Drive to picnic]

Woman: Here, I want you to meet my brother. This is Deedra and she's running for US Senate!

Brother: Oh, hi! I've heard so much about you!

Strategy vs Substance

Similar to not taking the bait and responding outside their expectations, in any given moment, you have to decide if the conversation is focused on strategy or substance.

A strategy might be to find common ground or leave them with something to think about.

Substance might be sharing true information or correcting a wrong.

Sometimes the strategy includes substance.

Sometimes it's just about correcting wrong information.

Because I know myself so well, I can quickly determine where I'm going – strategy, substance, or both – based on the "feeling" I get in the situation.

It's taken a lot of years to get to a place where I can do that on the spot.

My conversations are not always perfect, I still reflect on what I could do better with each conversation, but I almost always recognize the value of where I decided to go based on the energy of that moment.

The only "loss" is if I allow myself to forfeit my values due to what someone else says or does – particularly if that was their goal.

Man: Independents are [profanity] and won't vote for anyone that's not a Republican light in Arizona.

Me: Your opinion of Independents is the real reason we have such a hard time courting them as Democratic candidates. Independents are like the pretty girl at the prom that everyone thinks already has a boyfriend, so they're too afraid to ask her to dance. She doesn't care what letter you have on your jersey. She wants to know that you respect her, her mind, and her opinions... and that you will be honest in the relationship.

Man: The NFL is a private business. A private business can make their employees do whatever they want.

Me: Could a private business require employees to give a loyalty oath to... let's say a politician... in order to keep their job?

Man: Yes. If employees don't like it, they can quit.

Me: That sounds a lot like a dictatorship. People being forced to show political or national loyalty in order to have a job.

Man: It's called freedom. Companies have the freedom to hire employees that fit into their culture and fire those that don't.

Me: What happened to the idea of American individualism? The idea that we don't want to be controlled by others?

Man: We don't want to be controlled by the government!

Me: But you're okay being controlled by your employer?

Man: I can't talk to you! You're twisting everything!

[man storms off]

Man: The more you Democrats cry about things that people like Roseanne [Barr] say, the more we will take over Congress! It's freedom of speech! Deal with it!

Me: So, you agree with what Roseanne said?

Man: It doesn't matter! She has the right to say it!

Me: Yes, she does. My question is, do you agree that people of color are apes?

Man: It doesn't matter! She has the right to say it!

Me: And we as a society have a right to condemn what someone says. I can defend someone's right to say hateful things and simultaneously condemn what they say. That's how a civilized society works. That's what it means to stand up for your fellow Americans and the American principles we espouse.

Man: I'm a strict constructionist for the US Constitution. You interpret the words written there and nothing else.

Me: Words wrote a hundred years ago at a different time?

Man: Yes! You can't change the Constitution just because you don't like something in it!

Me: I agree the US Constitution is an incredible document, way ahead of its time, and I am in awe of the writers for being so forward-thinking considering the time they lived in... but the founders were not Prophets, and the US Constitution is not a divine document.

Man: You can't add words to the Constitution. If it's not there, it's not a right!

Me: The words weren't there to give women or people of color personhood either, but we updated it. That's what the founders meant when they described it as a living breathing document.

Woman: Do you believe in abortion?

Me: Yes, I believe liberty over your own body is the most intimate freedom imaginable.

Woman: So, you believe in murder.

Me: I don't believe the government should force pregnancy.

Woman: I know three women who were raped and chose to have their children.

Me: And I'm happy they had that choice. But neither you nor I, nor the government, has the right to take that choice away from another woman. That's a violation of personal sovereignty over our own body, the ultimate loss of freedom.

Woman: Ok. Well, it was nice talking to you. Good luck.

Me: You too!

Protestor: Every year, a bill comes up in Senate committees to designate the Muslim Brotherhood as a terrorist organization. Every year the Senate votes it down. Would you vote for it?

Me: I don't know. I haven't read the bill.

Protestor: Oh, come on! That's your answer? That's so like a liberal to avoid the issue!

Me: I would never comment or vote on a bill that I haven't read.

Protestor: Why haven't you read it? I have!

Me: There are hundreds of bills that haven't made it out of committee that neither you nor I have read. But why has the Senate voted against it, by the way?

Protestor: I don't know. That's a good question to ask them.

Me: Let me know when you find out.

Protestor: So, you wouldn't call the Muslim Brotherhood a terrorist organization?

Me: The US Senate is refusing to, and they have access to intelligence reports that you and I don't, so I'd like to hear their reasoning first.

Woman: How would you pay for healthcare for all?

Me: We're already paying for it, the money's just going to the profit for insurance and pharmaceutical companies instead of our health.

Woman: I have a friend in Canada, and she told me they have to wait three months for some procedures.

Me: I have a friend that died this month because he couldn't afford his cancer treatment.

Woman: Three months is too long.

Me: Death is worse.

Woman: Citizen's United already said corporations can give donations as free speech. It was a bad decision, but it's now the law.

Me: The Supreme Court said in the same case that Congress could require donation disclosure and limits like they do humans.

Woman: No. Congress can't limit the donations. That's settled law. They can require disclosure, though.

Me: The Supreme Court also said in a different case that political donations could be limited. Of course, Congress can pass laws limiting corporate donations. Otherwise, you're arguing that corporations can have more 'free speech' rights than humans. That's definitely not settled law.

Man: There's nothing you can do about Citizen's United. The Supreme Court already ruled on it.

Me: The Supreme Court also said, in the same case, that the legislature had the right to restrict the amounts and require public disclosure, just like the requirements for human donations.

Man: Oh, ya. I forgot you're a lawyer.

Me: You don't need to be a lawyer to read the case and see what the Court said. I'm confused why Congress hasn't done it.

Man: What do you think we should do about all the big things people are worried about now?

Me: Can you be more specific?

Man: Immigration.

Me: I'm an immigration attorney, so I can tell you there's a lot we need to work on. I believe we can regulate who comes into our country and still retain our humanity.

Man: How do we do that?

Me: Not putting kids in cages would be a good start.

Man: Why do you think we're doing that?

Me: The administration has stated they want people to be more scared of coming to the United States and losing their children than staying in the countries where they're afraid of dying.

Man: We shouldn't have to pay for these people.

Me: I agree. Current law allows people to submit an application for asylum, then get a work permit so they can work to support themselves while their application is in process. Instead, we've chosen to put them in detention centers where we taxpayers pay for their food, clothing, and shelter at inflated rates.

Man: Don't you think we're making it clear we don't want them here?

Me: But we're a country of laws, right? We have asylum laws and procedures on the books... not following them is new. We definitely shouldn't want to be a country that puts kids in cages.

STRATEGY VS SUBSTANCE

Man: Are you really trying to win or just making a point?

Me: I cannot imagine putting as much time, energy, and money as I am in this campaign just to make a point.

Protestor: What do you call God?

Me: God.

Protestor: No, what word do you use for God?

Me: In English, God.

Protestor: What is it in Hebrew?

Me: I don't know.

Protestor: Why don't you know?

Me: Cause I don't know Hebrew?

Protestor: Oh, ya, right. How come you don't know Hebrew?

Me: Cause I'm not Jewish.

Protestor: You were the attorney for Elton Simpson.

Me: Nope. I wasn't even out of law school when he was arrested.

Protestor: No. You were his attorney.

Me: No. You can't be someone's attorney when you are not an attorney.

Protestor: You defended him.

Me: No. Members of the community asked how to post bail, I told them how. And I would do the same for anyone, including you, accused of a crime because the US Constitution guarantees people the right to bail and a trial.

Protestor: Well, it's out there that you were his attorney.

Me: And yet I wasn't.

Protestor: Well, anyway, we'll let that one go, but....

Woman: What's the worst thing that's happened to you on the campaign trail?

Me: Having to give up cheesy eggs and grits from Waffle House due to their advocacy for weak labor oversight and because they kept calling the police on their Black customers.

Traits of a Tyrant

T he final tip I will share is that tyrants do exist.

They're dedicated to oppressing and over-powering you. To triggering you. To causing you pain.

The trick is to recognize them.

If you know someone's sole intent is to hurt you or cause you to lose yourself in your anger, you can choose, in that moment, to not let them reach their goal.

There is so much power in that.

Man: I don't disagree with what the girls did in Tempe [Mosque vandalism].

Me: Then you agree?

Man: No. You're twisting my words. I agree with what they did, just not how they did it.

Me: How should they have done it?

Man: Freedom of speech means they can yell at Muslims all they want. But they shouldn't have destroyed property. They should have stayed within the law.

A related video of the woman who vandalized the Tempe Mosque can also be found on YouTube – Deedra2018: "Love is more powerful than Hate on Phoenix streets."

Muslim: You can't really understand Islam unless you can speak Arabic.

Me: And yet 80% of Muslims in the world don't speak Arabic.

Man: I'm for free markets. It lets companies prosper, and consumers provide the regulation by moving their money when they don't like how a company acts. We don't need government involvement.

Me: Free markets only work when the consumer actually has the freedom to move their money. Major corporations actually limit competition, so in many industries, consumers don't have anywhere to go. Consumers also don't know when companies are poisoning our air, food, and water, much less have the capacity to hold them accountable. Governments have a moral responsibility to protect citizens from bad actors, whether they are individuals or corporations.

Man [Dispensary Owner]: We can't count off our expenses on our taxes because the IRS considers it to be trafficking.

Me: Yes, I am aware. I also included on my website that banking is difficult due to the federal laws conflicting with the state laws.

Man: Yes.

Me: That's why we need to decriminalize Cannabis on the federal level and leave it to the states.

Man: We're not pushing for that. It's not realistic.

Me: Why not?

Man: We'll never get it.

Me: That's the same argument with Healthcare for all. It's too hard, we won't get it, so let's not even try. How about we start pushing for what we want and compromise on that instead of giving up from the beginning?

Man: We're not going to get federal decriminalization of cannabis just because we have a majority of Democrats in [both houses of] Congress.

Me: Why not?

Man: Because the Democrats were a majority in 2010, and they didn't do it then.

Me: We didn't have legal medical cannabis in any state in 2010. Now we have that plus recreational cannabis in some states. 2018 is a totally different world than 2010. But what that world will look like is up to us. I'm not giving up.

Note: Arizona voters approved the legalization of small quantities of cannabis in 2020.

Man: People don't care about all these sexual issues [holding up my policy card].

Me: They do if their sexuality is under attack. I don't want the government in my bedroom, and I'm not even LGBTQ.

Man: I'm an old Democrat. I remember when Democrats used to focus on international policy. Now it's all about identity politics and sexual stuff.

Me: Identities and sexual freedom are under attack in the USA right now. If we don't focus on protecting our family, friends, and neighbors right here, right now, there won't be an 'us' to focus on international issues. We can multitask, but we can't ignore our own backyard.

Man: I'm really concerned about the direction our country is going.

Me: I can give you some good news. I've been hanging out with young people. They are so impressive. They really understand what the problems are for the environment, Net Neutrality, equal rights, education, and healthcare. If we include them in the process and excite them about the possibilities, we can make some real changes.

Man: From what I'm seeing, young people are really confused. They seem to be attracted to Socialism. I keep trying to make them understand they just have to look at East Germany to see the problems with Socialism. East Germany fell because Socialism doesn't work.

Me: Not to defend Socialism or anything... but East Germany was Communist. Communism is what fell.

Man: Do you have priorities when you get into the Senate or is that determined by the Democratic party?

Me: It's a combination, but I have already signed a contract that my first priority has to be working on dismantling Citizen's United so that corporations and special interests aren't controlling the decisions in Congress.

Man: What are some other priorities?

Me: Protecting the environment so that the poisoning doesn't kill us and protecting Net Neutrality, so we have the freedom to access information.

Man: The environment is important, but Net Neutrality is not even the top five. I work in Tech and know.

Me: People under 30 very much understand the importance of Net Neutrality. It is definitely one of their top five issues.

Man: When they reach 50 like me, they'll understand it's not.

Me: If data is not treated equally and everyone doesn't have equal access to the Internet, there will be no way for anyone to know how the environment is being poisoned or what to do about it.

Woman: What kinds of pressure have you put on these Arabs to sit down and negotiate for peace?

Me: What kind of pressure do you think I could have put on them?

Woman: I want to know what you've done to hold those Arabs accountable!

Me: We're talking about the leaders of Arab nations, right?

Woman: Yes.

Me: Nothing. I don't know them. I've never met them. I can't imagine what power you think an average American citizen has over the leaders of any foreign country. We're struggling to hold our own leaders accountable these days.

Woman: You're Muslim, and you're running for political office. You should have done something about those Arabs before you even thought to run!

Me: I agree that being a US Senator would provide a greater opportunity to meet with foreign leaders and have those discussions than any of us average Americans would. I can guarantee that as Senator, I would try harder to have those conversations than what we've seen from our current government leaders. I can also guarantee that I would never profit from the continued conflict like so many do, so I would actually be interested in helping all parties find common ground and work toward peace.

Man [at Pride parade]: You're a Muslim that supports Pride?

Me: Yes!

Man: Then why don't you fix the Middle East?

Me: The Middle East isn't my country, and my hands are a little full with fighting to protect LGBTQ rights in my own country right now. Have you seen the bills being presented to hurt you lately?

Man: Yes. But you need to fix the Middle East.

Me: One country at a time, man. Let's start with our own country. Maybe as a Senator, I can start those conversations.

Man: I don't trust candidates who jump into a race at the last minute. It shows a lack of planning, resolve, and commitment. And you haven't paid your dues.

Me: I got into this race in April 2017. I was the first candidate to announce. I think my resolve is proven by having attended more than 500 events all over the state before January 2018. But what dues are you talking about?

Man: You should have run for school board or city council and moved up to state legislature before running for a Congressional seat.

Me: That's not a legal requirement for the office. Nor is it how every office has been filled. I'm qualified and dedicated; that's what's required. Elected offices are service positions, not corporate advancement opportunities.

Woman: I love your campaign, and I want to help! I know so many people. We could get your signatures in a matter of days and really get your message out!

Me: That sounds great!

Woman: I have a legal case I want you to take.

Me: I'm sorry, I stopped taking clients in October 2016 to put all my focus on the campaign.

Woman: You can take this one case.

Me: Legal cases are literally people's lives and should have a top priority. I know I can't do that while I am running this campaign.

Woman: I won't help you unless you help me.

Me: .... *The number of personal and legal ethics violations you just suggested... are just too many for me to unpack right now.*

Woman: I guess you don't want to win.

Me: Not at the expense of my soul and freedom, no.

Woman: I already received my ballot and wanted to ask you something before I decide whether to vote for you.

Me: Sure!

Woman: Will you make saving big cats your number one priority in the US Senate?

Me: Protecting the environment, including our ecosystem and endangered wildlife, is part of my platform.

Woman: No. Protecting big cats has to be your number one priority for you to get my vote.

Me: I can promise you that it is important to me, but I won't lie to you and say that it takes priority over all other environmental issues, or kids in cages, or healthcare, or education, and several other issues that affect everyone.

Woman: Then, I will not be voting for you.

Me: Just curious. Has any other person running for any office told you that protecting big cats will be their number one issue?

Woman: I haven't asked anyone else.

Me: So, I lost your vote because I'm accessible and honest with you?

Woman: No. You lost my vote because I asked you a question, and I disagree with your answer.

Me: And yet, I was available for you to ask, and I told you my position even though it was obvious from the question what you wanted me to say. That translates to accessible and honest.

Woman: But I want you to protect big cats!

Me: And I'm not saying I won't. I'm saying I won't make it my number one priority. Which is what you asked.

Woman: You keep saying all those other countries in the world have Universal Healthcare like you think those countries are better. I know we live in the best country on Earth. If you don't think so, you can move.

Me: I love the United States. I don't love that my family, friends, and neighbors are dying because healthcare in the US is based on profit instead of health. Wanting to improve something is a good thing.

Woman: We're fine just the way we are. We don't need people like you trying to change things.

Me: Do you have healthcare?

Woman: Yes. I have Medicare.

Me: Good for you that the government set up a healthcare system generations ago that you benefit from now. It's time we did the same for future generations. Not to mention protecting Medicare now so you won't be yet another person I know who is without healthcare options.

Woman: I don't want to pay for other people... especially people who are lazy and don't deserve it!

Me: It's called living in a society. It's how we get roads, bridges, and fire stations that we all benefit from. Our taxes pay for that. Just like we pay for Medicare out of our paychecks all our lives. Just like everyone would love the opportunity to do if we could get insurance and pharmaceuticals to stop treating us as profit margins... like every other industrialized country already does.

Woman: All the Democrats are saying "families should be kept together" or "end family separation." It's better if you stay on message, so everyone understands what we're trying to accomplish.

Me: Soon, the administration will say they are doing exactly what we asked by keeping families together... in cages. Now is not the time to be timid.

Conclusion

As I mentioned before, winning or changing people's minds is never my goal. Finding common ground, giving the opportunity to reflect on information or perspectives, and not leaving the situation worse than I found it are always my goals.

Knowing my goals gives me flexibility in the moment as I focus on the situation, the words, and the person I'm having the conversation with – as well as the watchers and the impact my words can have on them.

My recommendations to help you begin finding your way of engaging with people who "make your blood boil" are:

http://EnneagramInstitute.com

http://16Personalities.com

https://globalleadershipfoundation.com/geit/eitest.html

https://www.psychologytoday.com/us/tests/personality/emotional-intelligence-test

Tongue Fu by Sam Horn

Take the Bully by the Horns by Sam Horn

Never Be Bullied Again by Sam Horn

Don't Think of an Elephant by George Lakoff

Techniques for having meaningful conversations are just that – techniques.

Some will work better for you than others.

Because, in the end, any conversation involves you, another person, a topic, and a situation.

And the only thing you can control in the mix is you.

Know you. Experiment. Practice.

And most of all, know what your goals are in any conversation.

About The Author

Deedra Abboud is a Phoenix-based attorney and author, featured in the book *Love Meets Life*. She is founder of the Global Institute of Solutions Oriented Leadership, a solutions-oriented mindset consulting firm, and highly respected for her community leadership and advocacy.

Deedra is a recipient of the Tempe Human Relations Commission 'Martin Luther King Jr Diversity Award' as well as the Phoenix Human Relations Commission's 'Living the Dream' award.

Deedra has run for political office and previously served as an elected Vice-Chair for the Arizona Democratic Party. She's been a guest on CNN, MSNBC, local ABC/NBC/CBS affiliates, and local radio stations for her unique perspectives on politics, community advocacy, and life.

Originally from Arkansas, Deedra happily lives with her husband of twenty-plus years in Scottsdale, Arizona, and is always willing to engage in uncomfortable conversations that can bring us closer together.

Made in the USA
Middletown, DE
24 February 2021